1 semester ACCESS CODE for

NATIONAL GEOGRAPHIC LEARNING | WADSWORTH CENGAGE Learning

Includes access to the eBook for National Geographic Learning Reader *Cultural Identity in America*

D1254094

This access code is valid for **6 months** from the date of registration. You will only enter it once to register. After that, you will log in to the eBook with the username and password that you created during the registration process.

Access Code

PPPHM3SP3KCBQS

NATIONAL GEOGRAPHIC LEARNING | WADSWORTH CENGAGE Learning

Australia • Brazil • Japan • Korea • Mexico • Singapore • Spain • United Kingdom • United States

Cultural Identity in America

Publisher: Monica Eckman

Acquiring Sponsoring Editor:
Kate Derrick

Project Manager: John Haley

Subject Matter Expert:
Tatiana Holway,
Columbia University

Assistant Editor: Danielle Warchol

Editorial Assistant: Maggie Cross

Media Editor: Cara Douglass-Graff

Marketing Director:
Lindsey Richardson

Marketing Communications
Manager: Linda Yip

Content Project Manager:
Corinna Dibble

Design Director: Bruce Bond

Manufacturing Planner:
Mary Beth Hennebury

Rights Acquisition Specialist:
Alexandra Ricciardi

Production and composition:
Integra

Text and Cover Designer:
Bruce Bond

Cover Image: Greg Dale/National
Geographic Image Collection

For product information and technology assistance, contact us at
Cengage Learning Customer & Sales Support, 1-800-354-9706.

For permission to use material from this text or product,
submit all requests online at **www.cengage.com/permissions.**
Further permissions questions can be e-mailed to
permissionrequest@cengage.com.

Library of Congress Control Number: 2012933144

ISBN-13: 978-1-133-60428-0
ISBN-10: 1-133-60428-5

Wadsworth
20 Channel Center Street
Boston, MA 02210
USA

Cengage Learning is a leading provider of customized learning solutions with office locations around the globe, including Singapore, the United Kingdom, Australia, Mexico, Brazil and Japan. Locate your local office at **international.cengage.com/region**

Cengage Learning products are represented in Canada by Nelson Education, Ltd.

For your course and learning solutions, visit **www.cengage.com.**

Purchase any of our products at your local college store or at our preferred online store **www.cengagebrain.com.**

Instructors: Please visit **login.cengage.com** and log in to access instructor-specific resources.

Printed in Canada
1 2 3 4 5 6 7 16 15 14 13 12

Table *of* Contents

About the Series

Cengage Learning and National Geographic Learning are proud to present the *National Geographic Learning Reader Series*. This ground breaking series is brought to you through an exclusive partnership with the National Geographic Society, an organization that represents a tradition of amazing stories, exceptional research, first-hand accounts of exploration, rich content, and authentic materials.

The series brings learning to life by featuring compelling images, media, and text from National Geographic. Through this engaging content, students develop a clearer understanding of the world around them. Published in a variety of subject areas, the *National Geographic Learning Reader Series* connects key topics in each discipline to authentic examples and can be used in conjunction with most standard texts or online materials available for your courses.

How the reader works

Each article is focused on one topic relevant to the discipline. The introduction provides context to orient students and focus questions that suggest ideas to think about while reading the selection. Rich photography, compelling images, and pertinent maps are amply used to further enhance understanding of the selections. The chapter culminating section includes discussion questions to stimulate both in-class discussion and out-of-class work.

A premium eBook will accompany each reader and will provide access to the text online with a media library that may include images, videos, and other premium content specific to each individual discipline.

National Geographic Learning Readers are currently available in a variety of course areas, including Archeology, Architecture and Construction, Biological Anthropology, Biology, Earth Science, English Composition, Environmental Science, Geography, Geology, Meteorology, Oceanography, and Sustainability.

Few organizations present this world, its people, places, and precious resources in a more compelling way than National Geographic. Through this reader series we honor the mission and tradition of National Geographic Society: to inspire people to care about the planet.

"Where do you come from?" How often have you heard this question—as commonplace a conversation starter as "What's your name?" A polite way of asking you to reveal something about yourself, it's also an opening for you to give a stranger a glimpse of who you are. On the face of it, the question isn't a probing one. Yet, it's hardly a superficial one either. Who you are and where you come from are, after all, fundamentally intertwined. Just as identities are formed in and by specific places, places are shaped by and for their inhabitants in ways that are both subtle and pronounced, and something we call "culture" contributes to and emerges from the mix.

As one of the largest and most populous countries in the world and one of the most geographically and ethnically diverse, the United States manifests this dynamic give-and-take process more prominently and more variously than anywhere else on the globe. And as more and more immigrants come here, adapting to conditions foreign to them, while altering character of the regions in which they reside, questions surrounding identity and culture in this country become more pressing at this time.

The National Geographic Society is paying attention to them, as it always has. With its aim of covering "the world and all that is in it," the magazine provides a rich archive of feature articles focused on the contemporary United States. As its writers and photographers investigate the physical and cultural characteristics of specific locations throughout the country, they put faces on forces of assimilation and diversification, make the multifarious realities of globalization palpable, concrete. Introducing readers to people and customs that may seem foreign, they shed new light on familiar American themes as well.

Hence, the articles gathered in this reader offer an exceptionally direct entree to issues surrounding identity and culture in the 21st-century United States. So do many undergraduate campuses by their very nature, as they bring students, staff, and faculty together from disparate locales, and the question of "Where are you from?" comes to be widely aired. While the answers will be as diverse as the campus itself, this reader will offer further contexts for students to reflect on them and help guide college writers through compositions in reply.

Comparison is, thus, one of the main rhetorical modes employed here. But then, so, too are description, definition, classification, cause and effect. Classroom debates and argumentative essays may be prompted by some questions. Others will direct students toward papers that analyze specific topics and reach for their critical insights and implications. Expository essays may be enhanced by personal experience or by research or both. And since the materials assembled from the *National Geographic Magazine* are so suggestive and the topic of this reader is so broad, further explorations accompany each article for students to pursue individually, in groups, or as a class.

Finally, although no reader on the subject of identity and culture in this country can presume to be comprehensive, inclusiveness must equally be in principle a goal. Toward that end, the text of articles has been edited for brevity and some images that originally accompanied them have been excluded. It is hoped that the necessity for such abbreviations in no way detracts from the articles themselves—that, on the contrary, the selections will augment appreciation for the differences and the commonalities amongst peoples living here and now, in the United States.

CHANGING AMERICA

As record numbers of immigrants arrive in the United States, a public high school in Virginia offers a window into the burgeoning diversity of the country and the challenges of acculturation. At the same time, it also suggests how a new generation of young adults is affecting what it means to be "American" at the beginning of the twenty-first century.

As you read "Changing America," you should consider the following questions:

- What are some characteristics that you consider to be specifically "American"? Do you find these in the article? Does Swerdlow note others that might supplement or modify your view?
- As you read "Changing America," bear in mind the date of publication – September 2001. What effects might 9/11 have had on the school subsequently?

An influx of immigrants, especially Asian and Hispanic, is changing the face of the United States—and the prom scene for students at a Virginia high school.

CHANGING AMERICA

Photographs by Karen Kasmauski

Pausing to pray during a private girls-only ice skating party, members of a Muslim youth group maintain their modesty. "Wearing the head scarf is a big challenge," says Fatima Abdallah, the group's 22-year-old coordinator. "People call us terrorists or foreigners. But most of us grew up here and are part of this society."

THE CURRENT WAVE OF
IMMIGRANT CHILDREN
IN U.S. SCHOOLS
IS REDEFINING WHAT IT MEANS TO LIVE
IN AMERICAN THE BEAUTIFUL.

J. E. B. Stuart High School opened in Falls Church, Virginia, in 1959. At that time the school, named for a famous Confederate cavalry commander in the American Civil War, possessed a student body of 1,616—virtually all Anglo-American. Change came slowly, accelerating during the mid-1990s, when immigration to the United States—legal and illegal—reached today's near-record level of a million people a year. According to the 2000 census, 10 percent of America's 281 million residents were born in other countries, the highest percentage since 1930 and the largest number in U.S. history. Before 1965 more than three-quarters of all immigrants to the U.S. came from Europe, owing largely to quotas that favored northern Europeans. In 1965 Congress removed those quotas, and since then more than 60 percent of immigrants have come from Asia, Africa, the Caribbean, the Middle East, and Latin America. Says Kenneth Prewitt, former director of the U.S. Census Bureau, "We're on our way to becoming the first country in history that is literally made up of every part of the world."

People have a natural right to life, liberty, and the pursuit of happiness.

Immigration patterns worldwide show a flow of people from poor countries to those with stronger economies, especially to industrialized countries with aging workforces. The influx is changing the makeup of populations in Britain, now 7 percent foreign-born, and France, also 7 percent. Immigrants now constitute nearly 10 percent of Germany's population, and 17 percent of residents in Canada are non-Canadian. In many ways J. E. B. Stuart mirrors this immigration revolution. Half of its 1,400 students were born in 70 countries.

In "Combating Intolerance," an elective course for juniors and seniors at Stuart, class discussions cover such topics as hate crimes, Ku Klux Klan violence, and why "No Irish Need Apply" appeared on job posters in cities where Irish immigrants looked for work in the 19th century. The morning I sit in, one of the students remarks: "America is a country of immigrants but also a country that sometimes hates immigrants."

Adapted from "Changing America" by Joel K. Swerdlow: National Geographic Magazine, September 2001.

"So why would anyone want to immigrate to the U.S.?" I ask, wondering if the students can reconcile this country's ideals with its shortcomings. Hands go up. "It's a country that gives people a chance to escape," a boy from Eritrea says. "People have a natural right to life, liberty, and the pursuit of happiness," declares a girl from Nicaragua. More hands wave. "What makes America special is that things are more 'wishable,' more likely to happen here," says a boy from Vietnam. "It's the tolerance," adds one voice. And then another: "The best way for us to learn tolerance is just seeing people of other cultures every day here." Heads nod in agreement.

They seem a little smug to me. "What's it like in this school for kids who don't speak English?" I ask. The class on intolerance is silent. "Do you ever do anything with them?" Someone in the back makes a comment, and the last row laughs.

Students in this class reflect a wide range of colors and cultures, but all speak English fluently and with no accent. Earlier that morning I'd eaten in the cafeteria and had heard many students who could not answer even simple questions from the people at the cash registers.

In 1990 some 32 million U.S. residents spoke a language other than English at home, and more than 7 million lived in households with no fluent English speaker over 14 years old. When language data from the 2000 census become available next year, the number of households with little or no English is sure to be much larger.

A basic command of English is a requirement for U.S. citizenship. Many argue that it also constitutes a foundation for economic self-sufficiency.

For the students who arrive at J. E. B. Stuart speaking no English, life can be tough. Two volunteers from "Combating Intolerance"

Beneath the sameness in fashion is a current of ethnic soul—a diversity that students cling to even as they conform.

escort me to a nearby corridor where English as a Second Language (ESL) is taught. "I *never* come here," says one. He was born in Pakistan but learned English when he came to the U.S. at age ten. "Yeah," adds the other boy, born in the U.S. but whose parents are Middle Eastern. "I haven't been here in years."

Ruth DeJong, who has taught ESL for 20 years, says, "About a fifth of the students now are nonliterate in their native language. That makes it much more difficult for them to learn English." A child's age of arrival in the U.S., she explains, is crucial. Young children have little difficulty with English, learning it in elementary school at the same time they learn to read. For many of the students in her class, who are beginning English and only starting to read at ages 14 to 17, it is much harder.

"Let's do some reading now," DeJong says, passing out a booklet written by local teachers. It contains reading and vocabulary lessons based on fictional students. "Many students are at school," reads one student. "They are talking and laughing. They are not talking to Ali. He is sad and afraid."

Slowly and softly, DeJong calls on everyone, even those who never raise their hands. She is both gentle and persistent. If they don't learn to speak and read English now, she knows, they won't stay in school—no matter how intelligent they are.

One-fifth of the full-time jobs in the U.S. pay eight dollars an hour or less. Filling most of these jobs are the 40 percent of the workforce who have no education beyond high school. Similar figures characterize most industrialized countries. For immigrants with poor language skills and little money, entering a technology-driven job market is increasingly difficult.

Flip through the 1964 yearbook from Stuart High School and you'll count 14 students with the surname Smith but none named Martinez or Nguyen. By 2000 there were only 6 Smiths, and 11 Martinezes and 23 Nguyens—an influx of Hispanics and Asians that echoes a natural trend.

J. E. B. Stuart's computer labs are furnished with up-to-date equipment. The teachers are patient, and students still struggling with English participate here along with everyone else, learning to use word-processing software and to cruise the Internet. I find Mel Riddile, the high school's principal, standing in the hall outside one of the labs, greeting each passing student by name.

"Maybe the key to success lies in computers," I suggest. Riddile disagrees. "Computers are important," he says, "but not as important as literacy. The kids have to be able to read or they can't even use computers," Riddile continues. "Here we spell hope 'r-e-a-d.' We make them 'haves' by teaching them to read. It's no guarantee, but it's essential."

Riddile shows me how reading programs permeate the school's curriculum. Students who need extra help attend a reading laboratory, but even in science and mathematics a systematic effort is made to teach reading. In the school's library, students seem to feel no social stigma as they select the easiest books.

Emphasizing that more than half of his students qualify for free or reduced-price meals in the cafeteria, Riddile describes efforts to keep them in school: 6 a.m. automated wake-up calls help, as do special counselors who speak foreign languages. But some still drop out, he says, because they either need to work or become too discouraged. Parents, unfamiliar with the inner workings of an American high school and sometimes illiterate in their own language, are ill-equipped to help their children succeed. "We're the best hope these kids have," says Riddile.

"It's as if you took the whole human race and threw it up in the air—and everyone ended up here," says Mel Riddile, principal of J. E. B. Stuart High School in Fairfax County, Virginia. Students come from some 70 different countries, and more than half of them must learn English as a second language. Stuart's seniors, posing here for their class portrait, often discover that post-graduation life can be much more balkanized—economically, ethnically, racially. "But at Stuart they mix," says Riddile. "Everybody's a minority here—and that's the best mix of all."

In the end Riddile is upbeat. Students who attend Stuart enjoy a special advantage, he says. "Going to school here makes them better prepared for the world. They're living in the workplace of the 21st century."

A visit to the counselors' offices offers further perspective on the workplace of the 21st century. "Immigrants often do the work no one else wants to do," says one of the counselors, referring to child care, housekeeping, and restaurant work. There is no shortage of such jobs in Fairfax County, Virginia, the jurisdiction that operates J. E. B. Stuart—where the median household income is $80,000 a year. "But students don't want these types of jobs. Their parents do this kind of work out of necessity, but most of the students hope to do something more professional."

"How many go on to college?" I ask.

"About 59 percent of the student body as a whole goes on to four-year colleges and 21 percent to two-year schools," another counselor replies. "But the numbers are much lower for foreign-born students. The big economic jump may be made by their children. Remember that many of the kids here have already passed through a great filter. They have a much better chance of making it than do lots who don't get here. It's relative. For them, to have a job and a home and enough money to feed a family can be a very big accomplishment."

Statistics about literacy and language and college prospects aside, what about being a teenager at J. E. B. Stuart—an immigrant teenager or an American teenager in this small-scale melting pot? A teenager with black skin or white skin, brown, yellow, or red skin—a teenager who speaks English or Spanish or Chinese or Hindi?

"I don't want to be white," says a white student from Poland. I'm in the library with a cross section of students who volunteered to speak with me.

Others agree with the Polish-born youth, but I'm confused. They explain. To call someone "white" is an insult, as are synonymous terms like Wonder bread. "I don't consider myself white," says a young woman from Russia. She has white skin. "Whites act white and do white stuff."

"What's 'white stuff?'" I ask.

"White kids act different. They hang out differently. Whites are privileged. They're smart, do homework on time, run the student government, participate in plays and musicals, sell stuff, have parents who are involved in the school."

"When you go to apply for a job," says one boy, "you have to act white."

"What do you do on weekends?" I ask. They all answer: Eat at a diner, talk, chill, watch television, go to an outlet mall, be with a boyfriend while he gets his car inspected, talk on the telephone, go to a movie.

"Sounds like what a white person would do," I say. Several students shake their heads, amazed at my inability to understand.

Most white students remain silent during these discussions. "I won't apologize for being white," says one.

I end up wondering if these kids aren't just struggling with an age-old adolescent dilemma: wanting to achieve versus wanting to be "cool." If achievement—or at least too much achievement—is unfashionable and achievement, as they have defined it, is "white," then "white" is not cool.

Whether they want to end up "white" or not, the kids here know they're in a blender:

I'm forgetting Arabic, I can feel it fading away, being sucked away from me.

People of different colors and textures go in, and a mixture that appears homogeneous comes out. Everyone has a backpack. Most boys wear jeans and T-shirts; many girls wear short skirts or tight pants, showing a bit of bare midriff. Boys and girls wear earrings and talk about the same music.

But running beneath the sameness in fashion and attitude is a current of ethnic soul—a diversity that many of the students cling to even as they conform. They may sense that they are losing their family stories in the blender. Students here come from places where there's war, civil unrest, or extreme poverty. Some have horrible memories; a few have seen family killed. Most of them, though, have asked their parents very little about their decisions to immigrate. "My parents don't talk much about it," one explains. Another girl says, "I'm Malaysian, but one set of my grandparents was from Thailand. I don't know anything beyond that."

The students' ethnic awareness coupled with the sense of losing their ethnic identity creates a subtle tension, even in the relatively benign atmosphere of the high school. "Hey, Italian!" evokes a response of "Hey, mulatto!" Pakistani girls are teased about wearing pajamas to school.

"I'm forgetting Arabic," says one student. "I can feel it fading away, being sucked away from me."

"It's part of becoming an American," says a friend.

This pattern persists even in the Hispanic community, which now constitutes more than 12 percent of U.S. residents. Roughly half of second-generation Hispanics assimilate so completely that they don't learn Spanish.

"We feel better with our own people," explains one student when I ask about apparently segregated groups in the cafeteria, which has a distinct geography that all the students can readily map out. Groups that sit together include Pakistani, *(Continued on page 12)*

MARYLAND

Falls
Church

Washington D.C.

VIRGINIA

© 2001 National Geographic Maps/National
Geographic Image Collection

Culture clashes rarely faze Stuart's
students but can unsettle their parents.

(Continued from page 9) Spanish-speakers, Moroccan, freshmen, cheerleaders, slackers, and nerds. Blacks who have recently arrived from Africa do not sit with the black Americans. Some tables are frequented by students who live in the same apartment building.

Despite such boundaries, most tables appear just plain mixed. At what looks like a typical table I pass out a piece of paper and ask everyone to write down his or her ethnic background. The results: "half Greek, half Middle Eastern," "Greek," "Saudi Arabian," "Bolivian," "African American," "Hispanic," "white (American)," "Russian," "African," "Pakistani," "confused," "mixed—black with??"

Lunch in the cafeteria seems dominated by interaction between two groups that transcend ethnic differences: boys and girls. Hand-holding, hugging, and occasional kissing have been very much in evidence throughout the school. Even some of the Muslim girls, who wear clothes that cover their entire bodies, have magazine pictures of muscular black men wearing only bikini briefs taped up inside their lockers.

What do these teenagers think of the cultural rules their parents try to enforce? A Sikh student says he finally talked his father into letting him cut his hair. Some of the Muslim girls argue with their parents about what kinds of dresses they can wear. One girl says that her mother told her she would have to marry an Asian man, and another girl insists that people must marry for love. A third girl reports that her mother says that people marry people, not cultures.

But most Stuart students are too young to be thinking of marriage. Conversations, especially among the boys, quickly turn to cars. "A car means freedom," one says. "You can go anywhere—your car is your life." A friend, who is saving his minimum-wage earnings for a car, says, "I know this girl farther out in Virginia I want to visit. With a car we could go to the shore or to New York. Doesn't everyone want to get away?"

At 2:05 p.m. the school day ends, and a rush to buses and cars begins. Some students get rides with parents or friends. Music blares from radios, kids sit on the grass, shouting, laughing, and flirting. I go for ice cream with several boys, most from the football team. It's a typical J. E. B. Stuart group: an African American, an Afghan Italian, a Cambodian, and a Palestinian. They're talking about rap music when two girls walk in. One of the boys goes over to talk to them. When he returns, the others tease him. He defends himself: "I just asked if they'd like to chill together sometime."

These are normal American teenagers, I think, wondering how I'll get them to discuss immigration issues. Then I realize that they've already taught me the most important lesson. Young people whose backgrounds span the spectrum of human cultures are becoming "normal American teenagers," and in the process they will change America. We may not know yet what the change will mean, but the kids themselves know they are at the heart of something significant. As one boy, speaking simply and confidently, told me: "We make America more interesting."

Discussion Questions:

- What appear to be the most important factors that contribute to one's identity, according to the high school students Swerdlow interviews? What appear to be the most important factors for him? Insofar as there are differences, are they generational? If so, what are the implications?

- While Swerdlow focuses on the cultural diversity beneath the fabric of sameness that characterizes the student body at Stuart, is that sameness--in clothing, in musical tastes, in what it takes to be "cool"--more than just superficial? In other words, to what extent do fashions reflect one's identity? Affect it?

- What are the qualities Stuart students associate with being "white"? In what ways is the term pejorative? Could it be a synonym for "American"? Or perhaps something more generic?

- Swerdlow identifies several fundamental tensions in the world of Stuart high school students, including the need to learn English and the fear that one's native language will be forgotten, as well as a consciousness of one's ethnic identity and a sense that it may be dissipating. How are these related to a dilemma faced by many teenagers, regardless of background--namely, the desire to fit in and the urge to be true to one's self?

Writing Activities

- You know the age-old question "What's in a name?" Taking it up, consider what names--first, middle, last, even nicknames--indicate about one's identity. As you do so, consider also what constitutes one's identity, and the extent to which names are representative of it.

- You also know the saying, "You are what you eat." What about "You are what you speak"? What are some ways in which the language(s) you speak express and/or suppress who you are?

- In 1913, Woodrow Wilson said: "The great melting-pot of America, the place where we are all made Americans, is the public school, where men of every race, and of every origin, and of every station in life send their children, and where, being mixed together, they are all infused with the American spirit and developed into the American man and the American woman." One hundred years later, is this idea still meaningful?

- Of all the holidays celebrated throughout the year, which two or three are the most important to you, and why? How are they related to your particular background, or not? Where do they fit, if at all, into the American landscape?

Collaborative Activities

- Following Swerdlow's example, take a poll of the ethnic backgrounds of the students in your classroom, and then compare the results with his. Is there greater or lesser diversity, or about the same? How do you account for the composition of your class? In what ways is it representative of "America"? Look up the most recent U.S. census, to help ground your discussion in facts.

- In looking at the images that accompany the article from the perspective of the post–9/11 world, how do you see them? What additional and/or different ideas and messages might they convey?

ZipUSA: NEW YORK, NY 10013; "AFTER THE FALL"

A year after the attack on Manhattan's World Trade Center on September 11, 2001, a firefighter and two neighborhood residents recall their experiences on that fateful day and reflect on the effects on their city and their lives.

As you read "After the Fall," you should consider the following questions:

- As you read the three accounts of 9/11, what feelings do you find dominant?
- Which feelings resonate with you?

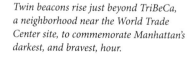

Twin beacons rise just beyond TriBeCa, a neighborhood near the World Trade Center site, to commemorate Manhattan's darkest, and bravest, hour.

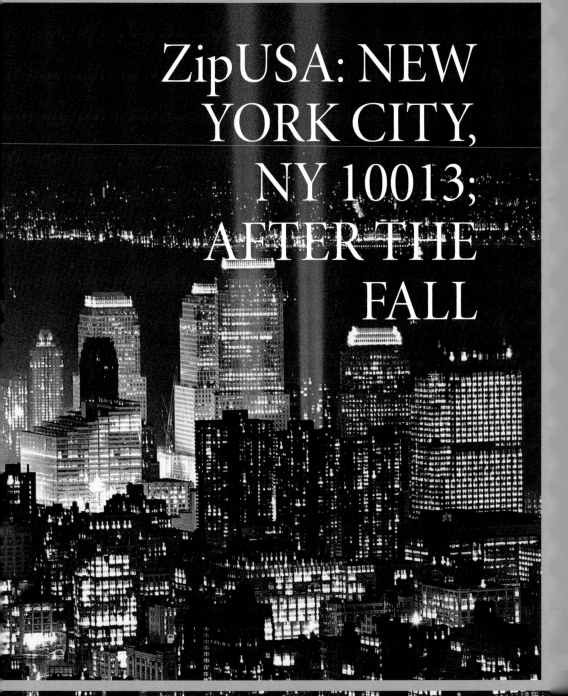

ZipUSA: NEW YORK CITY, NY 10013; AFTER THE FALL

Photographs by Ira Block

FOUR BLOCKS FROM THE WORLD TRADE CENTER (ZIP CODE 10048) ZIP CODE 10013 BEGINS. THE END OF 10048 IS TOLD BY A FIREFIGHTER

WHOSE HOUSE LOST 14 MEN ON SEPTEMBER 11.

TWO 10013 RESIDENTS FILL OUT THE TALE.

CANTO I: After the towers collapse, I arrive on the scene. There are no streets, only caverns of destruction, filled with sections of I beams, aluminum facade, dust, paper, and mud. Buildings surrounding what will come to be known as ground zero are gutted, burning fiercely, have hundreds of broken windows, or have been ripped wide open by flying girders. The command system is shattered; a chief is yelling orders from atop a rig. Every man seems to be from a different unit, and most lack basic equipment. We stretch hose lines to control fires in the acres of rubble, and pass stretchers, breathing masks, and forcible-entry tools over the girders to try to rescue trapped firemen.

Later I find my company, Ladder 15, at a staging area, where they've set up chairs outside the shattered windows of an office building's backside, like some war zone Parisian café.

After a few hours of awaiting orders, we split up to look for work. I find a large contingent of firefighters and police on the south side of Tower 2's remains, snaking a hose line into the rubble's smoky darkness. I search for

Only hours after the collapse of the towers, the recovery had begun.

victims under the wreckage. No sign of anyone.

From time to time the smoke lifts a little, showing six stories of uncollapsed steel girders and concrete flooring looming overhead. I keep searching, making mental notes of what girder I'll duck under if the rest of the building gives way.

Men shout for relief at the end of the hose line. I follow the line into intense heat and choking smoke. About a half hour later I reach the end and offer to take the nozzle, but the nozzleman refuses. "I'm not going anywhere until Duncan comes back!" he yells. By tradition, a company keeps the nozzle until the fire is out and firefighters from the house are safe. I help feed in hose, then start back to get some tools. Suddenly I feel sick and dehydrated. Hundreds of hands steady me as I clamber over rubble and down ladders that the brothers have laid across the steepest sections.

In the triage center in the firehouse across the street, the nurses seem like angels with IVs.

Adapted from "ZipUSA: New York, New York 10013; After the fall" by Noel Maitland: National Geographic Magazine, September 2002.

Before I fall asleep, I think back to the afternoon, when firefighters and construction workers fired up earthmoving equipment and started clearing the street. Only hours after the collapse of the towers, the recovery had begun.

—NOEL MAITLAND

CANTO II: You know my neighborhood. Last September, the sidewalk in front of my home became the backdrop for news reporters showing the world the devastation. My neighborhood, TriBeCa, just north of ground zero, also became a triage center when merchants threw open their doors to the injured and scared. It became a staging area for rescue workers searching for survivors in the smoldering rubble at the end of my street. And my corner was one where thousands streamed to pay final respects to those lost in a national tragedy that played itself out in an American neighborhood.

We had elementary schools and a canine day care center. We were also home to Miramax Films and some of the world's trendiest restaurants. We were an eclectic mix of artists, Wall Street brokers, and middle-class families. We are different now. Weary from the effort to recover and plagued by uncertainty, we are a neighborhood adrift.

Paul, a neighbor, was the son of "homesteaders," middle-class families attracted here by city subsidies after the towers were built in the mid-seventies. Like so many Americans, he decided to raise his own family where he grew up. A month after the attacks, he packed up and left. For how long? I asked. "Forever," he replied.

A friend from uptown offered to walk me home one night. As we walked down my street, he grabbed my arm in alarm. "I know that smell," he said, of the ever present smoke in the night air, reminder of the fires still burning deep inside that diminishing pile. "I grew up next to a cemetery," he

Last September, the sidewalk in front of my home became the backdrop for news reporters showing the world the devastation.

said. It was the smell of the crematorium.

I watched one morning as a father walked his son to school down my street. Once-proud skyscrapers stood vacant, their facades burned and stripped, their offices charred honeycombs. The son took his father's hand and asked, "Where is the future?" His father replied, "The future is everywhere around you, at all times."

—DIANA KANE

CANTO III: Weeks later, when the sirens had vanished from the night and we were no longer asked for passports, gas bills, and drivers' licenses to prove that we lived in what we came to call the frozen zone, everything looked the same and everything felt different.

My wife, Fukiko, and I were lucky. We had been across the street when Tower 2 came down with the roaring sound of a steel-and-glass avalanche. We were engulfed by that cloud of dust that rose 25 stories above the street, a cloud so opaque that it looked like a solid. The cloud was made of pulverized floors, exploded glass, smashed desks, computers, food, file cabinets, and human beings. She and I were separated in the dust, found our way home separately, and celebrated the simple fact of being alive.

We were lucky in another way: In our loft 14 blocks north of ground zero, we had electricity. Television, telephones, the Internet all worked. So did we. For nine straight days, we wrote newspaper stories about the calamity. On the tenth day I wrote nothing and for the first time sat on a couch, thinking about the ruined world, and wept.

But life also provided its own consolations. In the streets we met some of our neighbors for the first time. We stood on street corners together, manual laborers and dot-com workers, mothers and children, all staring downtown at the smoldering stumps of the towers. We asked about children, and dogs, and survivors. The emotions of awe, horror, rage were gone quickly, replaced by a shared sense of vulnerability.

That is what remains: vulnerability. And from vulnerability there has emerged a tough fatalism. We all learned, that terrible morning, that we could die while reaching for a piece of toast at breakfast. Where I live, that knowledge has made us more human. Even on streets noisy again with traffic, strangers say good morning. Men kiss their wives more, and hug their children, and walk with them to the Hudson to embrace the sunset. But not one talks with utter confidence about tomorrow.

—PETE HAMILL

Discussion Questions:

- How would you characterize each of the three voices in this essay? What distinguishes each one? What do they have in common?

- What lessons do these three New Yorkers take away from 9/11? In what ways might they be applicable more generally?

Writing Activities

- Given that a "canto" is a major division of a long poem, what does the arrangement of the article into three cantos suggest? What does this way of approaching 9/11 imply?

- What are some examples of recovery in this article? What specific senses of the word do they exemplify? As you consider and compare them, develop a definition of what "recovery" means.

Collaborative Activities

- What does living in a "post–9/11" world mean to each of the students in the classroom? Is there any common theme? Consider differences, too, and what their significance might be.

HIP-HOP PLANET

With roots in Africa and the slave trade, and with more recent sources in U.S. ghettoes, such as the South Bronx, hip-hop has become not only a global phenomenon but also a huge and lucrative industry. What makes hip-hop so appealing over time and across cultures, and what makes it so successful commercially are key questions asked by James McBride, a journalist, a jazz musician, and, until recently, an outlier from the "hip-hop planet" he describes.

As you read "Hip-Hop Planet," you should consider the following questions:

- At the beginning of this essay, McBride explicitly acknowledges a generation gap. Does it affect your response to his treatment of hip-hop?
- Similarly, McBride's racial background is also important, as he notes. How might your own figure in your reading of this essay?

The Bronx Two aspiring rap artists join fists near their home in the Bronx River Houses, one of the New York City public housing projects where the world-conquering mélange of music, dance, and graffiti known as hip-hop was born in the 1970s.

HIP-HOP
PLANET

Photographs by David Alan Harvey

AFRICA *Traditional drumming propels a newborn's welcoming ceremony in the Casamance region of Senegal. Powerful West African rhythms survived the slave trade and continue to pulse in the lands of the African diaspora, laying a foundation for many popular music forms: jazz, salsa, rock, hip-hop.*

AUTHOR JAMES MCBRIDE SEARCHES FOR THE
ROOTS OF THE MUSIC
THAT CAN'T BE IGNORED.

I live on a hip-hop planet.

This is my nightmare: My daughter comes home with a guy and says, "Dad, we're getting married." And he's a rapper, with a mouthful of gold teeth, a do-rag on his head, muscles popping out his arms, and a thug attitude. And then the nightmare gets deeper, because before you know it, I'm hearing the pitter-patter of little feet, their offspring, cascading through my living room, cascading through my life, drowning me with the sound of my own hypocrisy, because when I was young, I was a knucklehead, too, hearing my own music, my own sounds. And so I curse the day I saw his face, which is a reflection of my own, and I rue the day I heard his name, because I realize to my horror that rap—music seemingly without melody, sensibility, instruments, verse, or harmony, music with no beginning, end, or middle, music that doesn't even seem to be music—rules the world. It is no longer my world. It is his world. And I live in it. I live on a hip-hop planet.

Not since the advent of swing jazz in the 1930s has an American music exploded across the world with such overwhelming force. Not since the Beatles invaded America and Elvis packed up his blue suede shoes has a music crashed against the world with such outrage. This defiant culture of song, graffiti, and dance, collectively known as hip-hop, has ripped popular music from its moorings in every society it has permeated. In Brazil, rap rivals samba in popularity. In China, teens spray-paint graffiti on the Great Wall. In France it has been blamed, unfairly, for the worst civil unrest that country has seen in decades.

Its structure is unique, complex, and at times bewildering. Whatever music it eats becomes part of its vocabulary, and as the commercial world falls into place behind it to gobble up the powerful slop in its wake, it metamorphoses into the Next Big Thing. It is a music that defies definition, yet defines our collective societies in immeasurable ways. To many of my generation, despite all attempts to exploit it, belittle it, numb it, classify it, and analyze it, hip-hop remains an enigma, a clarion call, a cry of "I am" from the youth of the world.

Adapted from "Hip-Hop Planet" by James McBride: National Geographic Magazine, April 2007.

We'd be wise, I suppose, to start paying attention.

Hip-hop is a music dipped in the boiling cauldron of race and class, and for that reason it is clouded with mystics, snake oil salesmen, two-bit scholars, race-baiters, and sneaker salesmen, all professing to know the facts, to be "real," when the reality of race is like shifting sand, dependent on time, place, circumstance, and who's telling the history. Here's the real story: In the mid-1970s, New York City was nearly broke. The public school system cut funding for the arts drastically. Gone were the days when you could wander into the band room, rent a clarinet for a minimal fee, and march it home to squeal on it and drive your parents nuts.

The kids of the South Bronx and Harlem came up with something else. In the summer of 1973, at 1595 East 174th Street in the Bronx River Houses, a black teenager named Afrika Bambaataa stuck a speaker in his mother's first-floor living room window, ran a wire to the turntable in his bedroom, and set the housing project of 3,000 people alight with party music. At the same time, a Jamaican teenager named Kool DJ Herc was starting up the scene in the East Bronx, while a technical whiz named Grandmaster Flash was rising to prominence a couple of miles south. The Bronx became a music magnet for Puerto Ricans, Jamaicans, Dominicans, and black Americans from the surrounding areas. Fab 5 Freddy, Kurtis Blow, and Melle Mel were only a few of the pioneers. Grand Wizard Theodore, Kool DJ AJ, the Cold Crush Brothers, Spoony Gee, and the Rock Steady Crew of B-boys showed up to "battle"—dance, trade quips and rhymes, check out each other's records and equipment—not knowing as they strolled through the doors of the community center near Bambaataa's mother's apartment that they were writing musical history. Among them was an MC

The long history is that spoken-word of music made its way here on slave ships from West Africa centuries ago.

named Lovebug Starski, who was said to utter the phrase "hip-hop" between breaks to keep time.

This is how it worked: One guy, the DJ, played records on two turntables. One guy—or girl—served as master of ceremonies, or MC. The DJs learned to move the record back and forth under the needle to create a "scratch," or to drop the needle on the record where the beat was the hottest, playing "the break" over and over to keep the folks dancing. The MCs "rapped" over the music to keep the party going. One MC sought to outchat the other. Dance styles were created —"locking" and "popping" and "breaking." Graffiti artists spread the word of the "I" because the music was all about identity: I am the best. I spread the most love in the Bronx, in Harlem, in Queens. The focus initially was not on the MCs, but on the dancers, or B-boys. Commercial radio ignored it. DJs sold mix tapes out of the back of station wagons. "Rapper's Delight" by the Sugarhill Gang broke the music onto radio in 1979.

That is the short history.

The long history is that spoken-word music made its way here on slave ships from West Africa centuries ago: Ethnomusicologists trace hip-hop's roots to the dance, drum, and song of West African griots, or storytellers, its pairing of word and music the manifestation of the painful journey of slaves who survived the middle passage. The ring shouts, field hollers, and spirituals of early slaves drew on common elements of African music, such as call and response and improvisation. "Speech-song has been part of black culture for a long, long time," says Samuel A. Floyd, director of the Center for Black Music Research at Columbia College in Chicago. The "dozens," "toasts," and "signifying" of black Americans—verbal dueling, rhyming, self-deprecating tales, and stories of blacks outsmarting whites—were defensive, empowering strategies.

Paco Arias (in Cardinals jersey) escaped a world of gangs and violence when he moved from a rough Chicago neighborhood to suburban Dayton. The 14-year-old soon linked up with other teens who share his love of hip-hop, far from the conditions in which it arose.

ighways wrap around the city of Dayton, Ohio, like a ribbon bow-tied on a box of chocolates from the local Esther Price candy factory. They have six ladies at the plant who do just that: Tie ribbons around boxes all day. Henry Rosenkranz can tell you about it. "I love candy," says Henry, a slim white teenager in glasses and a hairnet, as he strolls the factory, bucket in hand. His full-time after-school job is mopping the floors.

Henry is a model American teenager—and the prototypical consumer at which the hip-hop industry is squarely aimed, which has his parents sitting up in their seats. The music that was once the purview of black America has gone white and gone commercial all at once. A sea of white faces now rises up to greet rap groups as they perform, many of them teenagers like Henry, a NASCAR fanatic and self-described redneck. "I live in Old North Dayton," he says. "It's a white, redneck area. But hip-hop is so prominent with country people ... if you put them behind a curtain and hear them talk, you won't know if they're black or white. There's a guy I work with, when Kanye West sings about a gold digger, he can relate because he's paying alimony and child support."

Obviously, it's not just working-class whites, but also affluent, suburban kids who identify with this music with African-American roots. A white 16-year-old hollering rap lyrics at the top of his lungs from the driver's seat of his dad's late-model Lexus may not have the same rationale to howl at the moon as a working-class kid whose parents can't pay for college, yet his own anguish is as real to him as it gets. What attracts white kids to this music is the same thing that prompted outraged congressmen to decry jazz during the 1920s and Tipper Gore to campaign decades later against violent and sexually explicit lyrics: life on the other side of the tracks; its "cool" or illicit factor, which black Americans, like it or not, are always perceived to possess.

Hip-hop has continually changed form, evolving from party music to social commentary with the 1982 release of Grandmaster Flash and the Furious Five's "The Message." Today, alternative hip-hop artists continue to produce socially conscious songs, but most commercial rappers spout violent lyrics that debase women and gays. Beginning with the so-called gangsta rap of the '90s, popularized by the still unsolved murders of rappers Biggie Smalls and Tupac Shakur, the genre has become dominated by rappers who brag about their lives of crime. 50 Cent, the hip-hop star of the moment, trumpets his sexual exploits and boasts that he has been shot nine times.

"People call hip-hop the MTV music now," scoffs Chuck D of Public Enemy, known for its overtly political rap. "It's Big Brother controlling you. To slip something in there that's indigenous to the roots, that pays homage to the music that came before us, it's the Mount Everest of battles."

Most rap songs unabashedly function as walking advertisements for luxury cars, designer clothes, and liquor. Agenda Inc., a "pop culture brand strategy agency" listed Mercedes-Benz as the number one brand mentioned in *Billboard's* top 20 singles in 2005. Hip-hop sells so much Hennessy cognac, listed at number six, that the French makers, deader than yesterday's beer a decade ago, are now rolling in suds. The company

> **E**veryone has the urge deep down to be a bad guy or a bad girl. Everyone likes to talk the talk, but not everyone will walk the walk.

even sponsored a contest to win a visit to its plant in France with a famous rapper.

In many ways, the music represents an old dream. It's the pot of gold to millions of kids like Henry, who quietly agonizes over how his father slaves 14 hours a day at two tool-and-die machine jobs to make ends meet. Like teenagers across the world, he fantasizes about working in the hip-hop business and making millions himself.

"My parents hate hip-hop," Henry says, motoring his 1994 Dodge Shadow through traffic on the way home from work on a hot October afternoon. "But I can listen to Snoop Dogg and hear him call women whores, and I know he has a wife and children at home. It's just a fantasy. Everyone has the urge deep down to be a bad guy or a bad girl. Everyone likes to talk the talk, but not everyone will walk the walk."

You breathe in and breathe out a few times and you are there. Eight hours and a wake-up shake on the flight from New York, and you are on the tarmac in Dakar, Senegal. Welcome to Africa. The assignment: Find the roots of hip-hop. The music goes full circle. The music comes home to Africa. That whole bit. Instead it was the old reporter's joke: You go out to cover a story and the story covers you. The stench of poverty in my nostrils was so strong it pulled me to earth like a hundred-pound ring in my nose. Dakar's Sandaga market is full of "local color"—unless you live there. It was packed and filthy, stalls full of new merchandise surrounded by shattered pieces of life everywhere, broken pipes, bicycle handlebars, fruit flies, soda bottles, beggars, dogs, cell phones. A teenage beggar, his body malformed by polio, crawled by on hands and feet, like a spider. He said, "Hey brother, help me." When I looked into his eyes, they were a bottomless ocean.

In Dakar, where every kid is a microphone and turntable away from squalor, and American rapper Tupac Shakur's picture hangs in market stalls of folks who don't understand English, rap is king. There are hundreds of rap groups in Senegal today. French television crews troop in and out of Dakar's nightclubs filming the kora harp lute and *tama* talking drum with regularity. But beneath the drumming and the dance lessons and the jingling sound of tourist change, there is a quiet rage, a desperate fury among the Senegalese, some of whom seem to bear an intense dislike of their former colonial rulers.

"We know all about French history," says Abdou Ba, a Senegalese producer and musician. "We know about their kings, their castles, their art, their music. We know everything about them. But they don't know much about us."

Assane N'Diaye, 19, loves hip-hop music. Before he left his Senegalese village to work as a DJ in Dakar, he was a fisherman, just like his father, like his father's father before him. Tall, lean, with a muscular build and a handsome chocolate face, Assane became a popular DJ, but the equipment he used was borrowed, and when his friend took it back, success eluded him. He has returned home to Toubab Dialaw, about 25 miles south of Dakar, a village marked by a huge boulder, perhaps 40 feet high, facing the Atlantic Ocean.

About a century and a half ago, a local ruler led a group of people fleeing slave traders to this place. He was told by a white trader to come here, to Toubab Dialaw. When he arrived, the slavers followed. A battle ensued. The ruler fought bravely but was killed. The villagers buried him by the sea and marked his grave with a small stone, and over the years it is said to have sprouted like a tree planted by God. It became a huge, arching boulder that stares out to sea, protecting the village behind it. When the fishermen went deep out to sea, the boulder was like a lighthouse that marked

the way home. The Great Rock of Toubab Dialaw is said to hold a magic spirit, a spirit that Assane N'Diaye believes in.

In the shadow of the Great Rock, Assane has built a small restaurant, Chez Las, decorated with hundreds of seashells. It is where he lives his hip-hop dream. At night, he and his brother and cousin stand by the Great Rock and face the sea. They meditate. They pray. Then they write rap lyrics that are worlds away from the bling-bling culture of today's commercial hip-hoppers. They write about their lives as village fishermen, the scarcity of catch forcing them to fish in deeper and deeper waters, the hardship of fishing for 8, 10, 14 days at a time in an open pirogue in rainy season, the high fee they pay to rent the boat, and the paltry price their catches fetch on the market. They write about the humiliation of poverty, watching their town sprout up around them with rich Dakarians and richer French. And they write about the relatives who leave in the morning and never return, surrendered to the sea, sharks, and God.

The dream, of course, is to make a record. They have their own demo, their own logo, and their own name, Salam T. D. (for Toubab Dialaw). But rap music represents a deeper dream: a better life. "We want money to help our parents," Assane says over dinner. "We watch our mothers boil water to cook and have nothing to put in the pot."

He fingers his food lightly. "Rap doesn't belong to American culture," he says. "It belongs here. It has always existed here, because of our pain and our hardships and our suffering."

Some call the Bronx River Houses the City of Gods, though if God has been by lately, he must've slipped out for a chicken sandwich. The 10 drab, red-brick buildings spread out across 14 acres, coming into view as you drive east across the East 174th Street Bridge. The Bronx is the hallowed holy ground of hip-hop, the place where it all began. Visitors take tours

Hip-hop comes full circle on a beach outside Dakar. Jally, a kora-playing griot who makes a living telling stories at ritual ceremonies (or for tourists), jams with Omar N'Gala Seck, a rapper who infuses the American form with fresh shots of its African roots.

through this neighborhood now, care of a handful of fortyish "old-timers," who point out the high and low spots of hip-hop's birthplace.

It is a telling metaphor for the state of America's racial landscape that you need a permit to hold a party in the same parks and playgrounds that produced the music that changed the world. The rap artists come and go, but the conditions that produced them linger. Forty percent of New York City's black males are jobless. One in three black males born in 2001 will end up in prison. The life expectancy of black men in the U.S. ranks below that of men in Sri Lanka and Colombia. It took a massive hurricane in New Orleans for the United States to wake up to its racial realities.

That is why, after 26 years, I have come to embrace this music I tried so hard to ignore. Hip-hop culture is not mine. Yet I own it.

Much of it I hate. Yet I love it, the good of it. To confess a love for a music that, at least in part, embraces violence is no easy matter, but then again our national anthem talks about bombs bursting in air, and I love that song, too. At its best, hip-hop lays bare the empty moral cupboard that is our generation's legacy. This music that once made visible the inner culture of America's greatest social problem, its legacy of slavery, has taken the dream deferred to a global scale. Today, 2 percent of the Earth's adult population owns more than 50 percent of its household wealth, and indigenous cultures are swallowed with the rapidity of a teenager gobbling a bag of potato chips. The music is calling. Over the years, the instruments change, but the message is the same. The drums are pounding out a warning. They are telling us something. Our children can hear it.

The question is: Can we?

Discussion Questions:

- What makes hip-hop a uniting force—and for whom? How can it also be divisive—and in what ways?

- What happens when countercultural phenomena such as hip-hop go mainstream? Does the sting get dulled? Does complicity in the institutions and conditions that hip-hop critiques invalidate the message?

- In what ways does hip-hop transcend racial differences, especially in the United States? In what ways does it reinforce and even exploit these differences? Which tendency seems more prominent? More significant? Why?

- While one crucible of hip-hop is the South Bronx, another is Senegal. How does McBride navigate between the two? What does hip-hop's becoming such a global phenomenon further suggest?

Writing Activities

- "Hip-hop remains an enigma," says McBride, and yet it is also "all about identity." How are the two statements contradictory? How are they complementary?

- Do you consider yourself a member of the "hip-hop planet"? If so, what draws you to it, and what do you gain from it? If not, why not? And what are the ramifications?

- "'It's just a fantasy,'" says one young man of the glorification of violence, crime, and sexual abuse that some of the more popular and commercially successful hip-hop conveys. Do you agree? And even if it is mere fantasy, is it necessarily innocuous when it comes to the real world?

- Concluding the essay by re-emphasizing the importance of hip-hop to a generation younger than his, McBride says the music is "telling us something. Our children can hear it." Do you yourself hear it? What might that something be? How might you convey the message to your elders—if at all?

Collaborative Activities

- Choose several examples of hip-hop music as a class, divide into groups accordingly, discuss the lyrics and the rhythms of your group's sample, and then compare notes amongst yourselves and in relation to the "hip-hop planet."

- What two or three songs are at the top of the charts in your world today? What genre(s) do these fall into? What do you think accounts for their popularity?

ZipUSA: PAWTUCKET, RI 02860; HOME FAR AWAY

While only about one third of Cape Verdeans currently live on the islands of the West African archipelago, a significant population of immigrants has come to Pawtucket, Rhode Island. As "Home Far Away" describes what draws Cape Verdeans to the old mill town, the article also explores ideas of "home."

As you read "Home Far Away" you should consider the following questions:

- What is your idea of home?
- What does "homelessness" suggest to you?

Born in Cape Verde, Africa, but living an ocean away, Ildebranda Oliveira tends bobbins for $7.50 an hour at Stretch Products in Pawtucket. She misses her homeland's weather and food, but not its poverty: "Over there there's no jobs. Over here I work and make money."

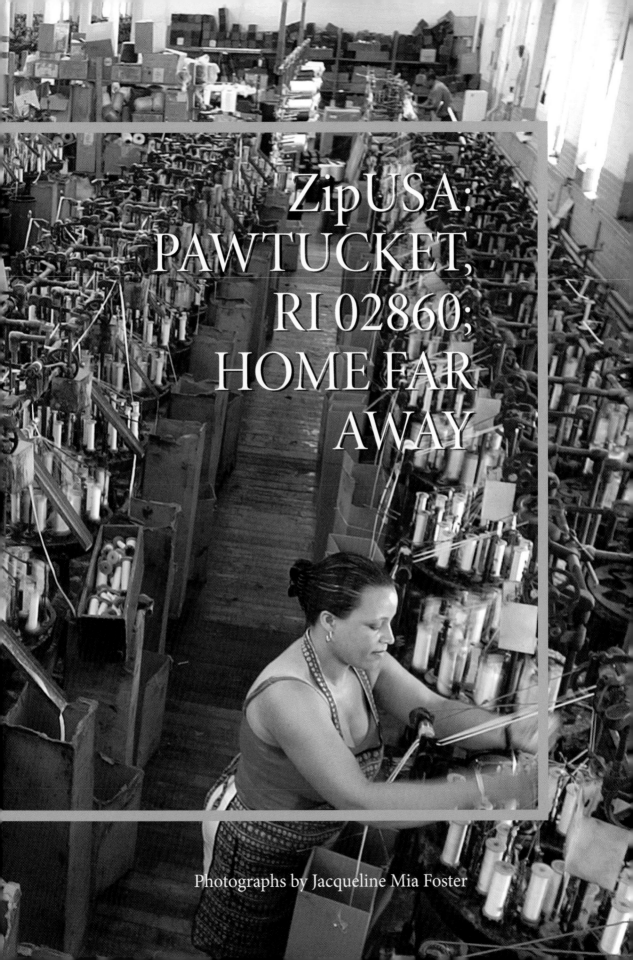

ZipUSA: PAWTUCKET, RI 02860; HOME FAR AWAY

Photographs by Jacqueline Mia Foster

Pulonga'l Bita (playing accordion) jams with his band; Cape Verdeans may leave the islands, but the islands don't leave them, lingering in music and memory.

THE PROMISE OF A BETTER LIFE

ENTICES CAPE VERDEANS TO DREAM AGAIN.

A few blocks from the river of traffic on I-95 that cuts Pawtucket in two, from the fast-food restaurants, gas stations, and motel that light otherwise dark streets, lies a snug bright club called Cantinho, where Cape Verdeans retreat from the rush and regrets of their adopted home. On a Saturday night, well-dressed men and women, their skin ranging from dark chocolate to coffee flooded with cream, drink amber-colored *grogue*. The room buzzes in Kriolu, a blend of Portuguese and West African languages that slaves arriving from the 15th to the 19th centuries created in Cape Verde, 10 islands some 400 miles off the coast of Senegal. On the walls hang pictures of a white sand beach, a packet boat that carried Cape Verdeans fleeing drought and poverty to New England early in the 20th century, and Amílcar Cabral, the revolutionary who fought for the country's independence from Portugal in 1975.

One of Cantinho's owners, Jack Galvão, left the Cape Verdean island of Brava in 1979 at 17, part of an exodus triggered by fear that the islands' economy would be driven to collapse by a post-independence swerve to the left. He arrived in Rhode Island with three years

We don't have anything bigger than love. Love is bigger than the sea and sky.

of high school English, took a factory job, and worked his way through college. Now a successful accountant and real estate agent, he still yearns for the land of his birth. "In Cape Verde you don't buy yourself a drink," says Galvão, "your friend buys you a drink." As if on cue, he asks the bartender to pour some grogue for a man across the room.

A guitarist begins to play, backed by a bass and a keyboard, and the club fills with the music of the islands and their far-flung diaspora—languid, dreamy songs called *morna* and faster counterparts called *koladera*. Soon one of Galvão's friends, João Alfredo, takes the microphone.

Walking out between the tables, he fixes his gaze on a seated woman, then gestures with an upraised palm to another. "We don't have anything in the world bigger than love," he croons. "Love is bigger than the sea and sky."

The crowd applauds and joins in: "Tell me, my love, which way is the sky? The sky is in

Adapted from "ZipUSA: Pawtucket, Rhode Island 02860; Home Far Away" by Karen E. Lange: National Geographic Magazine, June 2004.

your breasts and in your black eyes."

A simple love song, perhaps, but it's part of a larger, more complicated romance: the bittersweet nostalgia of self-imposed exile. *Sodadi*, Cape Verdeans call it—longing. Or *triste alegria*—sad happiness. Economic necessity may have driven them from their home and keeps them from moving back, but their hearts remain in the islands. "It's wanting to stay but having to go," Galvão says. "It's sad because you're leaving, but happy because you're going to opportunity."

Cape Verdeans have been coming to Pawtucket in increasing numbers since U.S. immigration quotas were raised in the 1960s, drawn by manufacturing jobs and affordable rents. Most of Pawtucket's Cape Verdeans work in factories housed in 19th-century textile mills, live nearby in clapboard homes erected for earlier generations of immigrants, and grow flower and vegetable gardens as an echo of the family plots they left behind. If they can afford the airfare, they return home in the summer. If they can't, they return through music you hear everywhere in the neighborhood: The melody of a live guitar, or tunes on a Cape Verdean radio program, drifting out of a kitchen window; drumbeats as members of the Sons of Brava social club grind corn for a festival honoring São João Baptista, Brava's patron saint; CDs of songs recorded locally, then sold worldwide.

Pulonga'l Bita and his band, Amigos para Sempre, lounge on an old sofa in a cramped basement studio after recording traditional African-influenced roots music called *batuque* and *funana*. It's the music of poor country people, so unvarnished it was forbidden in pre-independence Cape Verde. "If you played that in the city, the Portuguese was going to put you in jail," says accordionist Zito'l Code, who performs to the metallic beat of a *ferinhu*—an iron bar tapped and scraped with a butter knife.

Bita, who looks a little like a hip-hop star—with his earrings, backward baseball cap, and

> **I**f they can afford the airfare, they return home in the summer. If they can't, they return through music you hear everywhere in the neighborhood.

upside down sunglasses—describes batuque on his home island of São Tiago. "The people go like that," he says, alternately slapping one thigh and then the other to produce a muffled snap that resembles the canter of a far-off horse. "And they dance all night."

Bita has turned batuque to contemporary themes in a series of songs about a Cape Verdean immigrant who is rejected by a girl because of his poor English. One hit the top of the Cape Verdean charts, but Bita still hasn't given up his day job as a landscaper.

Late one afternoon, while Bita is still at work, the mother of his children, Regina Garner, slices green bananas and manioc in their two-story walk-up for the family's dinner of fish stew. She isn't hungry herself, having eaten at McDonald's on the way home. Garner arrived in Pawtucket in 1989 with $20 in her pocket. The same day, she found work in a factory and a $300-a-month apartment. Slowly she built a life, one of happiness tinged with sorrow. Triste alegria. "I miss people, especially my father.... But over there you can't take care of your kids the way you want." Garner earns $15 an hour as a restaurant cook, a job that has scarred her forearms with burns.

Out in the driveway the couple's sons, ten-year-old Wilson and three-year-old Harrison, are playing basketball. In the dining room Garner's cousin Maria Lourdes Silva, visiting from Cape Verde, sits with a new baby boy, watching a music video: Bita and the band playing batuque in downtown Providence surrounded by women shaking their hips to the beat. Silva's baby is 12 days old, born just after she arrived in Pawtucket. She timed the trip so he would be an American citizen. Inspired by a place mat of U.S. presidents (and his and his brother's own names), Wilson named his baby cousin Kennedy. The infant begins to fuss, and Silva settles him into her arm and taps out batuque on his foot: the music of memory, the music of survival, the music of faraway home.

Discussion Questions

- *Triste alegria:* How do Cape Verdeans define this feeling? In what ways might it be applicable to other immigrant groups? How about the U.S.-born children of these immigrants? Is it a feeling that would resonate for them?

- What are the main characteristics of the Cantinho Bar? What do these say about the community?

Writing Activities

- In what ways is music politically charged for Cape Verdeans? In addressing the question, consider the culture of hip-hop as it is described here, and in comparison to "Hip-Hop Planet," another article in this reader?

- How are the different foods types noted in this article related to specific experience of immigrant Cape Verdeans? In what ways does the idea of a "melting pot" apply, or not?

Collaborative Activities

- What does the "American Dream" mean to you, individually? How would you define it collectively, as a class?

ZipUSA: OKLAHOMA CITY, OK 73106;
LEMONGRASS ON THE PRAIRIE

Oklahoma City may be a far cry from Saigon, but since the 1970s waves of Vietnamese have been settling there, creating a Little Saigon on the prairie, building new lives and retaining old customs.

As you read "Lemongrass on the Prairie," you should consider the following question:

- In which ways do in which "Asian" and "American" diverge and connect?

ZipUSA: OKLAHOMA CITY, OK 73106; LEMONGRASS ON THE PRAIRIE

Photographs by Penny De Los Santos

Waiting on tables in a Vietnamese restaurant.

GIVING BACK. HOLDING ON. MOVING UP.
IN OKLAHOMA CITY, SECOND GENERATION
OLD WORLD VIETNAMESE TRADITIONS
CLASH WITH A AMERICAN VALUES.

In our family we grow up to be a doctor or else.

A sense of the surreal swirls up like prairie dust as you drive through Oklahoma City and pull up to the flat, sprawling intersection of 23rd Street and Classen Boulevard. Just ahead hovers a giant golden geodesic dome, built by a local bank in 1958. Across the street, atop a trapezoidal hut, stands a 15-foot-tall white milk bottle (emblazoned with a pink ice-cream cone). A couple of blocks beyond rests a Gothic church, its enormous stained-glass windows sheltered by carved gray stone.

Somehow it's not where you'd expect to find a thriving community of Vietnamese, locally known as Little Saigon, the fragrance of lemongrass, garlic, and hot chili paste drifting out from a garish string of strip malls. Ten minutes away from the intersection, the heart of Little Saigon, you can easily walk to five restaurants specializing in *pho* (the classic Vietnamese beef broth soup), two Asian supermarkets, and several Chinese barbecue cafés.

The afternoon Loan Nguyen arrived in Oklahoma City in August 1980 remains as fresh as yesterday. Having left a refugee camp in Thailand, Loan, her husband, Thuong, and four children walked down a set of steel stairs onto the roasting tarmac at Will Rogers World Airport:

"It was hot," she remembers, "like going into the stove." Thuong had been a bone surgeon in Vietnam, and within two years he taught himself enough English to pass relicensing exams and undergo retraining as a family physician. Loan found a job with Coca-Cola, selling soft drinks to Asian convenience stores. In 20 years they have put four of their six children, plus a son-in-law, through medical school.

Thuy, an elegant, feisty young woman, is the eldest of the four doctor children. "In our family you grow up to be a doctor or else," she says, taking a break between patients in her two-room office a half mile down 23rd from her dad's. When she and three siblings were in high school earning straight A's, they were expected to concentrate on homework; the television was to be on just an hour each night. To enforce the rule, Thuong encased the television in a plywood box so that after the hour was up he could padlock it shut. Thuong and Loan still live in the same one-story brick house they bought for cash 17 years ago, two

Adapted from "ZipUSA: Oklahoma City, Oklahoma 73106; Lemongrass on the Prairie" by Frank Browning: National Geographic Magazine, March 2003.

Ha Ngo and Khach Pham bring groceries home in a cart, not a car.

doors from a nearly identical house where he keeps his office. Thuy lives in a two-story, upscale suburban house half an hour away.

"I don't want to live in an old, small house," Thuy says. "I'm living the American dream. We grew up poor. We want to move up in society."

That tension between the bonds of tradition and the blandishments of the American dream sizzles all across Little Saigon. Stop by Su Nguyen's Hop Ky café most any morning around 10 and, if you speak Vietnamese, you can hear Su trading stories with his old military buddies about their grandchildren and the mistakes that lost the war. One large South Vietnamese flag is tacked to a wall, another flies in the wind outside, and a third sits beside the Stars and Stripes atop an old deli case stocked with pig intestine, roast duck, and stuffed buns.

Three veterans in their 60s sip tea with Su. All, like him, went to prison for several years after the fall of Saigon; some spent more years in refugee camps.

"They come here every morning; some are retired, others work night shift. It's a good place to talk and remember," Su says through my interpreter, Khanh Tang, a young Vietnamese-American police officer. Su arrived in Oklahoma City with the second wave of Vietnamese refugees in 1991. Most of the people who now live in Little Saigon came about the same time. The first wave, who were placed here by Christian refugee agencies in the '70s and '80s, have mostly moved to the suburbs. "The rich move out and poor stay in town," Tang says.

Two nights later in his patrol car, Tang inches along the small side streets of Little Saigon, lined with simple frame bungalows. He flashes his spotlight into the yards, most tidy, a few with backyard junk.

"I wouldn't want to raise my son around here when there's drug dealing, prostitution, shooting just down the street," Tang says, referring to a seedy neighborhood nearby. Even closer is one of the most exclusive square miles in Oklahoma. The possibility of either encroaching on Little Saigon has spurred community leaders to build up the neighborhood's civic institutions. When the golden dome was in danger of being razed, a committee of longtime Oklahomans launched a "save the dome" campaign. Their effort seemed hopeless until Irene Lam, who is one of several thousand Chinese in the city, offered to buy it to create an Asian cultural center.

"Asian people are always looking for public space to have community meetings, and there was nothing here," she says, taking me on a tour of the building. "Now we can have cultural displays, music, dance, there's so much open space."

A shrewd businesswoman, Lam quickly lined up enough retail businesses that rents would easily pay off the building's 1.1-million-dollar asking price. Lam also understood the cultural and political value of saving this icon of Oklahoma life: "We could say it's a way for Asian people to give something back to Oklahoma City for the good fortune they have had here."

Giving back. Holding on. Moving up. These are old issues among immigrants to the United States. Part of the attraction of Oklahoma City is its scale. Orange County, California, where the first flood of refugees arrived after the fall of Saigon, now is home to 135,000 Vietnamese; nearly as many live in greater San Jose. Housing prices in both are higher and urban tensions more severe. Still, the sprawl that is Oklahoma City casts families and friends apart. Loan Nguyen has watched her three oldest children move away, something that would be unthinkable in Vietnam. The children badger her and Thuong to move out of Little Saigon, to join them in the suburbs away from the "crime," but the parents say no.

"Our idea is anywhere crime can happen," Loan says. "Soon we will be too old, and our children not stay with us. When we are alone, it is very convenient to walk to Vietnamese stores. It is more comfortable to be alone here."

Discussion Questions

- What is Dr. Thuy Nguyen's version of the "American Dream" and how does it not only differ from but also correspond with her parents'? How do these compare with other "American Dreams" in this reader?

- In what ways, and for whom, is Little Saigon a refuge? In what ways, and for whom, is it the opposite? How do these attitudes relate to identity? How do they affect the area itself?

Writing Activities

- A "television encased in a plywood box": this is one of many images of enclosure in this article. What are others? What is involved in each case, literally? Figuratively? What are the implications?

- "Giving back. Holding up. Moving on. These are old issues among immigrants to the United States," writes Frank Browning. How and to what extent do these issues resonate with the Vietnamese described in this article? What about other refugees, in contradistinction to immigrants generally?

Collaborative Activities

- Find out more about Oklahoma City, its history, and demographics, and reconsider the history and demography of Little Saigon in this context.

ONCE UPON A TIME IN LAREDO

A debutante's ball honoring Martha Washington has been a tradition in this South Texas border town since 1939. As Mimi Swartz details the customs of the event, as well as its costs, she looks at what unites and what divides Anglos and Mexicans in Laredo.

As you read "Once Upon a Time in Laredo," you should consider the following questions:

- What is your reaction to the idea of a debutante's ball? As you read the article, are your views modified?
- Is speaking a language other than English important in your world? What does being bilingual imply to you?

Perfect as porcelain dolls, debutantes and their escorts are formally presented to 1,500 paying guests at the Laredo Civic Center, in a ritual designed to preserve the established social order.

ONCE UPON A TIME IN LAREDO

Photographs by Penny De Los Santos

No deb goes it alone: As Alyssa Cigarroa waves during Saturday's parade, her cousin Nicholas Martin tosses beads to the crowd.

PART TEXAN, PART MEXICAN, AND SOMEWHAT AMERICAN, THE RESIDENTS OF LAREDO, TX. HAVE

LEARNED TO LIVE IN TWO WORLDS,

ACCEPTING BOTH AND JUDGING NEITHER.

The world of the Texas-Mexico border has always been inscrutable to outsiders. Consider the pageant presented by Laredo's Society of Martha Washington—part of a month-long celebration of George Washington's birthday, held since 1898. The notion of honoring our founding father and his kindly wife a stone's throw from Mexico seems almost comical. It's hard to associate that particular George W. with the dry, dusty scrub of South Texas. Laredo's blocky Civic Center, where local debutantes are presented in an annual and very lavish tribute to Mrs. Washington, is a far cry from the serene repose of Mount Vernon. Yet the ability to take a leap of faith into another world is what the border has always been about. Those who make the place their home know how to live in at least two worlds, accepting both and judging neither.

So on a blustery Friday night in February, a stage has been transformed into a replica of the Washingtons' drawing room, right down to the twinkling crystal sconces and the pale green, period-hued walls. Seventeen local

Yet the ability to take a leap of faith into another world is what the border has always been about.

belles make their debuts, teetering across the stage in elaborate gowns while a narrator praises Martha Washington's simple virtues with a solemnity that would satisfy the finickiest member of a First Family of Virginia.

But because this is the border, the first First Lady is extolled bilingually: Martha was *"la primera dama de nuestra nación,"* who "put her country and the General above herself." And, also because this is the border, there is something just a bit zany about the celebration. When you combine the psyche of wealthy Mexico with that of wealthy Texas, more is always going to be more. Debs in New York might display their well-practiced curtsies in spare white gowns and gloves, but these girls make their bows in dresses of gleaming satin and thick velvet, so encrusted with ruffles, beads, and lace that they elicit gasps from the audience. Two notable Laredoans have been

Adapted from "Once Upon a Time in Laredo" by Mimi Swartz: National Geographic Magazine, November 2006.

chosen to portray George and Martha, and on this, supposedly the President's last night in office, the First Couple's life is reenacted, with the debutantes and their escorts all playing roles. As each young woman is introduced, violins or the U.S. Army fife and drum corps playing, it is noted whether her mother or grandmother or great-aunt made her debut as "a Martha," whether her father or grandfather or great uncle ever played George Washington, and whether she or her escort—from an equally fine old family—was ever an "*abrazo*" child: Every year a boy and a girl from Laredo embrace their counterparts from across the border in Nuevo Laredo on the International Bridge before a huge, cheering crowd, epitomizing the love that people on both sides have for each other.

And so life has gone for more than a century here, where the cultures have not so much collided as colluded to form one region, separate and apart from both home countries. The two Laredos, it has been said, beat "with one heart." This particular stretch of border is both baroque and byzantine, the most stratified and status-conscious of border towns, part Texan, part Mexican, and somewhat American, with rules, rituals, and folkways that have grown as complex and vibrant as the bougainvillea that blooms along columns and rooftops in so many local yards.

It would be easy to make fun of Laredo and its pageant. In these days of war, famine, global warming, and the ever growing divide between rich and poor, an elaborate tribute to Martha Washington by debs wearing gowns that weigh 85 pounds and cost in the neighborhood of $30,000 is something of an easy target. Recently, however, change has come to the region—in the form of

Anglo immigrants, if they wanted to advance, became "Mexicanized." "Josephs" became "Pepes," learned Spanish, and, if they were lucky, married into the Mexican gentry.

drug violence across the border and, emanating from Washington, battles over immigration—threatening a way of life that has persisted here since the first Spanish settlers arrived in the 1700s. This year, despite the jeweled gowns and effusive abrazos at the celebration, it was natural to wonder whether Laredo's oldest families were honoring the past or clinging to it. And that didn't seem funny at all.

Alyssa Cigarroa had always dreamed of becoming a Martha. At 17, she is a beautiful young woman with shimmery brown hair, dancing eyes, and a wide, dazzling smile. She began reading the annual Sunday supplement featuring the debutantes when she was five. At seven her grandmother, Barbara Flores Cigarroa, took her to her first pageant. But wanting to be a Martha and actually becoming one are two very different things. None of the women on the Cigarroa side of the family had ever participated in the pageant, and in the rules governing this societal ritual, precedent can be a formidable obstacle.

Though the Martha Society's past president, Veronica Castillón, makes joining the organization sound as easy as sending in an application—"It's not complicated," she says blithely—women can spend up to eight years on the society's waiting list so their daughters can be selected as debutantes by longtime members. Some women are never picked at all. The ones who are come mostly from a small, elite group of old families. People like Linda Leyendecker Gutierrez and her sister, Jennie Reed—heirs to an oil-and-gas fortune bounteous even by Texas standards. Their grandfather played George Washington in 1905; both women are married to the men who were their pageant escorts; and their daughters made their debuts a few decades later.

For the families who take part, the cost of the event—the gown, the myriad parties—is not an issue. Nor is it discussed: "Would you ask me how many acres I own?" is Linda Gutierrez's practiced reply to any financial inquiry about the ball, equating it with the ultimate ranching faux pas. Over time, the price of a dress has escalated in direct proportion to the affluence of the ruling families: A beaded, velvet gown from the 1970s looks ornate until you see one from the post-NAFTA years, when the wealth of Laredo—and the inclination to show off that wealth—increased exponentially. Linda, whose stress-induced, *Exorcist*-like transformation during the event is a source of local legend, knows better than most how the richest people in town love to wear their hearts, their histories, and even their bankbooks, on their sleeves. "I want my daughter to steal the show," is the order one mother gave Linda. In Spanish, of course.

To understand Laredo's Martha Washington pageant, you have to understand the city's past. At best, Laredo is an acquired taste. It is one of those spots where it's best to develop an affinity for the sky because the land isn't much to look at. It is flat and scrubby, unsuitable for hardly anything but grazing, and the climate is hot and dry for most of the year. Laredo's appeal comes not from its topography but from its place on the map, its closeness to Mexico. Here, everyone is bilingual, and everyone switches languages with idiosyncratic abandon. ("I'm hearing about Shelby's party *todavía!*") A classic, bustling Mexican plaza is bordered by the lovely San Agustin Cathedral and the old La Posada hotel. Laredo's downtown streets smell of diesel exhaust and roasted *elotes*—ears of corn. Its old-fashioned awnings shield pedestrians in business suits as well as beggars in rags from the heartless sun.

In many ways, Laredo's upper class has changed little in more than 300 years: It is still dominated by preoccupations with lineage and class. Jennie Reed reminded me more than once that her family dates back to the 18th century. The city was founded in 1755 by a Spanish rancher who named Laredo after a town in Spain. Land on both sides of the Rio Grande was subsequently granted to people who were then citizens of New Spain, now Mexico. This world was socially stratified, with immigrants of Spanish descent at the top, and mestizos, mulattoes, and Indians below. Members of the lower classes were expected to address their betters as *don* and *doña*, partly out of respect and partly because they were beholden to them—the patrons were the only employers in town. They grew rich from ranching, running their small fiefdoms as they pleased.

After the U.S. defeated Mexico in 1848 in a bitter war for control of Texas, the boundary between the two countries shifted to the Rio Grande, and Laredo joined the Union. Those who wanted to remain Mexican citizens moved across the river to what became Nuevo Laredo—the new town. As commerce between the U.S. and Mexico increased, Laredo grew, drawing immigrants from Europe and other parts of the U.S. The area became even richer when oil and gas were discovered in the 1920s, and when the Mexican Revolution sent many from the wealthy, educated class scurrying for shelter on the U.S. side of the border. Laredo was a natural destination because, unlike in other Texas border cities, the early Spanish families had held on to their land and remained in power. They elected the officials, controlled the banks and businesses, and set the social tone. Anglo immigrants, if they wanted to advance, became "Mexicanized." "Josephs" became "Pepes," learned Spanish, and, if they were lucky, married into the Mexican gentry.

Community leaders created the first George Washington's birthday celebration as a way to gin up patriotism along the border during the Spanish-American War in 1898—to prove that Laredo's loyalty was to the U.S. With the addition of the Martha Washington Society in 1939, the Colonial Pageant and Ball became a way to connect the city's most eligible belles with its most eligible bachelors, cementing and maintaining dynastic alliances.

The result is a melting pot of Mexicans and Europeans. "We were a UN before there was a UN," Jennie Reed says. In a place like Manhattan or Boston, a debutante from a minority group is an anomaly. Here the girls' names resonate with the region's history: Treviño, Echa-varría, Vela, and de Anda, as well as Leyendecker, Averill, and Bruni. The oldest Mexican and Anglo families intermarried so long ago that no one in their right minds would attempt to make ethnic distinctions. Laredo is a modern case study for those who worry that the constant influx of Mexican immigrants threatens to divide the country into two cultures, two peoples, two languages. If this city's history is any guide, assimilation is a given, especially among those fortunate enough to rise to the top.

Meanwhile the social stratification continues: The rich have stayed rich, and the poor—owing to a cheap and plentiful supply of labor across the border—have stayed poor. Today the poverty level of Webb County, where the city is situated, is 31 percent, double the statewide average. Per capita income in Laredo is only $11,000. It is for this reason that many find the extravagance of the Martha celebration disturbing, as it puts on display a kind of wealth that has preserved itself for centuries on the backs of the poor. "Does the oligarchy think about the plight of the immigrants?" asks María Eugenia Guerra, a former debutante who publishes an alternative newspaper called LareDOS. "Only when it inconveniences them." Not surprisingly, Jennie Reed disagrees: "Of course we are aware of the poor here. People in the society probably give away more money to charity than

anybody. But if people who've worked hard want to spend their money this way, why not let them do it?"

When Alyssa Cigarroa finally crossed the stage for her debut, in a lavender gown encrusted with beads and sequins she'd helped design, the crowd whooped, perhaps because they sensed she represented a change in the order of things. You wouldn't think the Cigarroa name would be an obstacle to becoming a Martha. To be a Cigarroa in South Texas is to be something like a Kennedy, only without the tragic curse. At the turn of the 20th century, the family had substantial wealth in Mexico, but that wealth—in mining—was seized during the revolution. After that, Alyssa's great grandfather, Joaquin G. Cigarroa, Sr., worked his way through medical school, became an accomplished physician, and in 1937 settled with his wife in Laredo. The Cigarroas exhibit the values that have long contributed to the success of Mexico's most honorable families: Loyalty, service, and education take precedence over wealth for its own sake. Alyssa's grandmother, Barbara Cigarroa, still presides over lunches with her ten children, all of whom attended Ivy League schools (mostly Harvard) and became professionals (mostly doctors).

But even though Alyssa's father, Ricardo Cigarroa, a cardiologist, is perhaps the most important physician in town, Alyssa's desire to be a Martha was problematic. The story is convoluted, the truth impossible to discern. Whether it had to do with vague accusations of jealousy toward the family, a business feud among local doctors, or simply the Marthas' tradition of giving preference to members' daughters first (her mother, Lisa, was still on the waiting list), Alyssa's participation in the pageant was far from certain. That she was exemplary—as the Martha rules require—was not in question; it was just that the Marthas already had selected their debs for the year. It took a palace coup, engineered by a few members of the society, to get her chosen. After much politicking and a special vote, in the end the Marthas made room for Alyssa. "It was a revolution," is the way one member put it.

A revolution, of course, had already arrived— it had only taken old-line Laredo this long to notice. In the past, the city's wealthy Mexican-American residents had to create their own world because they weren't so welcome everywhere else. Though they traveled back and forth across the border to Mexico, no one visited Manhattan or Europe with the frequency they do now. It wasn't long ago that, even just a few miles up the road in San Antonio, people with Spanish surnames endured varying degrees of discrimination. The best law firms, the best hospitals, the San Antonio city council and mayor's office were all controlled by Anglo men. To succeed and prosper, it was best to stay home.

Those limitations have fallen away. The irony of Alyssa's deep desire to become a Martha is that a modern girl like her doesn't need the status anymore. Yes, weeks after the ball, her gown was still displayed on a mannequin in the Cigarroa family living room. And she enjoyed the parties given over the past year, at least five honoring each girl. These included a fete devoted to designer purses, one to designer shoes (Manolos were in evidence), a disco party, a Hollywood party, and, Alyssa's favorite, the one her grandmother gave her, in which the decor—tables, bows, lace—was a study in pink.

But, like the other debs, Alyssa has been raised to be a member of a much larger world.

What these girls want, in becoming Marthas, is not to cement their places in Laredo, but to carry a bit of Laredo with them into futures that will be much more complicated than that of their mothers and grandmothers.

She attended Manhattan's Parsons School of Design and spent a summer studying art in Paris. These young women have résumés to rival students at Andover and Exeter. One pursued independent study at Cambridge University, and another participated in an MIT engineering program. One young woman plans to major in genetics, another to become a radiologist, another to work at ESPN. What these girls want, in becoming Marthas, is not to cement their places in Laredo, but to carry a bit of Laredo with them into futures that will be much more complicated than that of their mothers and grandmothers.

Laredo itself has become a much more complicated place in their lifetimes, as a bloody drug war across the border threatens to spread north. The easy, open world of their childhoods is disappearing before their eyes. Where once the Marthas celebrated across the river after their debuts, the party this year was held in Laredo. "We don't go over there anymore" is a phrase heard frequently, and with good reason: Nuevo Laredo's annual homicide toll reached 46 shortly after the pageant. For Laredo residents, the possibility of getting caught in the cross fire is very real, as is the risk that their children could be kidnapped. "Three more die in N.L." was the headline in the *Laredo Morning Times* a few days before the ball.

Also in the headlines was a call to seal off the borders to keep out illegal immigrants, maybe even build a wall between the U.S. and Mexico, a move that would forever change Laredo. This is, after all, a town where the economy depends on immigrants who come to work and shop. "This place is so far removed from reality," says María Guerra. "If their housekeeper couldn't come, they would throw fits at what it would cost" to pay standard rather than border wages, she says. "But they bury their heads in the sand" when it comes to the current debate on immigration.

Sealing the border doesn't seem like such a bad idea to some, especially now that their daughters, as moneyed and well educated as any New England WASPs, no longer look to Mexico as their wider world but can move freely about the globe, with more opportunities than they could possibly explore in their lifetimes.

The usual parade honoring George Washington's birthday took place the day after the ball. The weather was bleak and cold, but the old families had set up shop in parking lots, barbecuing on flatbed trucks as they always did, while the hoi polloi sat on lawn chairs below, snacking on elotes and Domino's pizzas. It was a classic border scene, with the differences between rich and poor both obvious and ignored, as everyone begged for candy and plastic beads from the floats with the pretty girls in their jeweled gowns. But change was in the air, from both sides of the border, and these girls knew it, snuggling deep into their furs to ward off the chill.

Discussion Questions

- "Those who make the place their home know how to live in at least two worlds, accepting both and judging neither." How does the article substantiate this view of Laredo? Are there ways in which it brings the point into question?

- What specific processes of assimilation have characterized Laredo? In which direction do these tend to go? And what are the implications, in terms of both American and non-American culture?

- What kind of "change in the order of things" does the inclusion of Alyssa Cigarroa in the Martha ball suggest? What other, broader changes does it reflect and imply?

- Taking the point further, do you think the pageant is likely to endure much longer in the 21st century? Do you think it a valuable tradition worth preserving in some fashion? Or an archaic custom, best abandoned altogether?

Writing Activities

- How does the ball bring people together? How does it exacerbate differences? Which force is more powerful, and why?

- How does Laredo's Martha ball compare to a high school prom elsewhere in the country? In what ways are Laredo's "Martha's" similar to and different from other female prom-goers? What about brides? What kinds of ideas of "femininity" are implied?

- Do you think that an expenditure of $30,000 on one dress for a single occasion is justifiable? As you construct an argument for or against, take into account what your opposition might say, and try to place the issue in relation to broader American social, economic, and political values.

- What fantasies does the Martha ball fulfill? What realities does it reflect? How do fantasies and realities diverge? How do they interact?

Collaborative Activities

- Consider the role of gender in this article and in your response to it. What do the men in the classroom think about the Laredo pageant? Are the issues raised alien or familiar? What about the women in the classroom? Is there a gender divide? Either way, what are the implications?

- Immigration, always a vexed topic in this country made up largely of immigrants, has become even more so in recent years, especially on the Mexican-American border, but also in other locations and contexts as well. What are some of the issues at stake, and how do you navigate them in your class?

SILICON VALLEY: INSIDE THE DREAM INCUBATOR

A crucible of the high-tech industry, Silicon Valley not only wired the world but also made connectivity a condition of private and public life. As Cathy Newman examines how the inventors drawn to Silicon Valley realized some of their wildest dreams, she also situates their aspirations and achievements in relation to the broad concept of the American dream.

As you read "Silicon Valley: Inside the Dream Incubator," you should consider the following questions:

- What does the phrase "California lifestyle" suggest to you? How does it compare to the work-style of Silicon Valley?
- How are the technological tools you use a part of your day-to-day life and what would happen if you couldn't use them for, say, a week?

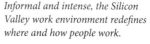

Informal and intense, the Silicon Valley work environment redefines where and how people work.

SILICON VALLEY: INSIDE THE DREAM INCUBATOR

Photographs by Bob Sacha

Million-dollar houses rose as fast as stock earnings in Silicon Valley during the technology-driven boom of the late 1990s. With the area's abundance of rich customers and shortage of lots, a developer in Cupertino could place luxury homes near a power substation and still draw buyers. Modest houses in the Valley came with $400,000 price tags. When the stock market fell last year, creating bankruptcies and layoffs, the housing market sobered up. For the first time in years sellers were accepting bids at or below asking price.

SILICON VALLEY,
THE EDGE OF THE FUTURE
OR THE PRECIPICE OF DESPAIR?

Silicon Valley thrives on risk.

A small earthquake hit Palo Alto my second day in town. The bedside lamp vibrated, nothing more, but it was a reminder that the San Andreas Fault snakes down this part of California.

Several days later Jim Calzia, a geologist with the U.S. Geological Survey, drove me out to see the San Andreas, which translates on the landscape as a low green trough. The Big One is predicted sometime in the next 30 years, Calzia said. It could be a 7 in magnitude: utterly catastrophic.

"So why do people still live here?" I asked.

Calzia barely suppressed a grin.

"How lucky do you feel?" he said.

Silicon Valley thrives on risk. Ever since 1933 when Frederick Terman, a professor of engineering at Stanford University, mentored two undergraduates named Bill Hewlett and Dave Packard, the Valley has been about placing bets on people, ideas, and inventions. Terman's protégés would go on to found Hewlett-Packard, the Valley's pioneer high-tech company.

Since then Silicon Valley has attracted the best and brightest from all over the world. It has as intellectual capital two great universities: Stanford and the University of California at Berkeley. It is home base to a who's who of technology and the incubator for hundreds of graduates seeking to emulate Hewlett and Packard. It was here that Pong, the first video game, went from dream to reality, as well as the ink-jet printer, the video recorder, the mouse, the personal computer, and much else we take for granted in the information age. The expertise of Silicon Valley has, in no small measure, wired the world.

At its high-flying peak in 2000, 43 of *Forbes* magazine's 400 richest Americans lived here. Their wealth added up to an estimated 184 billion dollars, and if you believed the hype, 60 new millionaires were minted each day. Dot-com fever fueled the jackpot economy; secretaries cashed in options and drove off in Porsches.

But in the opening months of 2001 the headlines wept financial woe. The Nasdaq, the technology-heavy stock index, had plunged more than 50 percent from its high a year earlier.

Adapted from "Silicon Valley: Inside the Dream Incubator" by Cathy Newman: National Geographic Magazine, December 2001.

Dot-coms foundered and sank. Even solid companies like Cisco, Intel, and Hewlett-Packard hoisted warning flags of workforce cuts and lower earnings. To add insult to injury, a power crisis had erupted in California. Blackouts stunned the state. You could build the fastest, smallest, most powerful computer, plug it in, and nothing happened.

Still the mood in the Valley registered optimistic, as if the water supply were fluoridated with Prozac. "We call it techno-optimism," said Jan English-Lueck, a professor of anthropology at San Jose State. "There's an addiction to opportunity, and if you don't see it that way, why are you even here?"

Silicon Valley is not a piece of official geography but a nickname for a 1,500-square-mile piece of northern California that runs from the outskirts of San Francisco south through Santa Clara County. It is an extended suburb of flat monotony, except for the expensive green idyll of residential areas such as Portola Valley and the grandeur of Stanford. Silicon Valley is an interior geography, a terrain made visible by grace of fluorescent and halogen light, connected by concrete tentacles of freeway.

"What would you show someone who came to visit Silicon Valley?" Chuck Darrah, a professor of anthropology, and his colleagues at San Jose State asked in a study of Valley families. "Yosemite, Monterey Aquarium, and Lake Tahoe," they'd respond. "Yes, but they aren't in Silicon Valley," Darrah would point out.

There is the weather, which for much of the year consists of unbroken blue sky and moderate temperatures. The relaxed lifestyle has made khakis and a shirt the business uniform of choice. The live-and-let-live mind-set

> There is an addiction to opportunity, and if you don't see it that way, why are you even here?

means anything goes. You are free to dye your hair blue, be openly gay, bare your navel ring at work, start a multimillion-dollar company. No one bats an eyelash.

"Think Florence with numbers," Morton Grosser, a consulting scientist based in Palo Alto, had said by way of explaining Silicon Valley. Instead of painters and sculptors, the Valley has geeks and nerds, and they are as passionate about circuitry as Michelangelo was about marble.

A computer whiz said he built an Altair 8800, one of the first do-it-yourself computer kits, because "it was cool and I wanted one."

Les Vadasz, an executive vice president at Intel, said that for an engineer the excitement is the project. "You know that what you are working on is ahead of the curve, ahead of everyone else. It's a sport. A game."

In his living room overlooking San Francisco Bay, Roger O'Neill showed me a metal box the size of a hatbox. O'Neill, a biochemist, is vice president of research and development at a small company called Guava Technologies. The box, he explained, is a type of flow cytometer. Simply put, it peeks inside a cell to see what's going on: to discern how, for example, a cell is reacting to a certain antibiotic. The instrument is not new, but because of the technology this particular model is one-twentieth the size of its competitors and more affordable, he said.

Explain the kick, I asked. He walked me over to a shelf over the mantle. "My grandfather and father built model trains," he said. He showed me a locomotive and cars. The detailing was exquisite—from the planks on the siding of the boxcars to the wheel spokes on the locomotive, and it was all made by hand. "This was something they did purely for the joy of creating," he said. "It's

A decent technician's wage in the computer industry can't keep John Singh and his young family out of a homeless shelter in San Jose. Between them Singh and his wife, a registered nurse, earn $105,000 a year. Yet exorbitant rents and a dispute with a landlord left the Singhs and their three children little choice but to move into a room at the Boccardo Reception Center, a former General Electric office complex that serves as San Jose's largest shelter. More than 40 percent of the shelter's residents have jobs.

not necessarily designing something from scratch that thrills me. For me the thrill comes from innovating within a basic design and making something beautifully that performs its purpose."

Silicon Valleyspeak has its roots in the language of business and engineering. You maximize your child's skill set, and if he plays in three different basketball leagues (as some do), there is value added in that his teammates' parents may turn out to be CEOs of companies you might be interested in. Vacation is downtime, but hardly anyone leaves a cell phone or handheld at home.

VCs are venture capitalists, the financiers of Silicon Valley. They round up the capital—from pension funds, wealthy individuals, and universities—needed to underwrite a fledgling company. Last year venture capitalists in the Valley invested an estimated 17 billion dollars in new companies, known as start-ups.

"Great cities are born because of the discovery of gold or oil because of geography and the location of a port," Grosser said. "The natural resource here is brains."

Despite the intellectual firepower of the Valley, I kept feeling a nagging sense of something not quite right, a subterranean rumble of something I couldn't put words to.

Maybe it was the dozens of Mercedes and BMWs in the student parking lot of Palo Alto High School, knowing the principal drives a 1991 gray Nissan truck. Or hearing one too many stories about the guy with a Mercedes and four-bedroom home who crybabied because he hadn't cashed in on the dot-com boom like his zillionaire buddies. Perhaps it was the 25-year-old who worked at Yahoo! who, when I expressed the hope my 15-year-old son would always know his way around a library, told me with faint disdain I should stop treating books like fetishes.

Maybe it was standing under the trees at the Drop-In Center run by the Urban Ministry in downtown Palo Alto, where homeless men and women turn up each morning for a cup of coffee directly opposite Stanford University and the high-end stores in the Stanford Shopping Center.

Besides providing a list of resources ("Where to take a shower," "Where to get medical help"), volunteers hand out 20 bus tickets each day, first come, first served.

"The bus tickets are very important to these men," Sergio Samame, a caseworker, explained, as a line formed under the shade of a metal overhang.

"Why?" I asked.

"They have nowhere to sleep. So they ride the bus all night."

Gentlemen, ladies. Attention please. Palm Pilots in hand? Business cards in reach? Ready? Set? We are going to *network*.

Rule number one. Opportunity surrounds you.

A meal with friends? Heads up. Case the room. Isn't that *Steve Jobs* at the next table? Your daughter's school play? Why not? CEOs have daughters too.

Visit the University Café in Palo Alto, Buck's in Woodside, or Il Fornaio in San Jose. Look around. See the two guys at that table? The kid who looks like a high school sophomore is hoping to do a start-up. The older guy is a venture capitalist. They are *cutting a deal*. The group of twentysomethings in the corner drawing on a legal pad? They are devising a business plan. Your turn. Pull out your cell phone. Establish that you too are a player.

"Everyone," said the anthropology professors Chuck Darrah, "is perpetually on the make."

In Silicon Valley money is, with few exceptions, not inherited. It is earned, either by invention of a brilliant idea or, sometimes, by the clever marketing of a mediocre one.

"When people make money, the first thing they want is a really nice house," said Paul Conrado, a high-end contractor based in Saratoga. His job is to build them those really nice houses. "Ego builds some of these homes," he said, as we took off to see his work. "I have 12 houses going at the moment. The lowest is going to cost a million and a half, the highest is over four million, and that's not including the cost of the land. Eleven clients are paying cash."

"We're also building a thousand-square-foot barn costing $400,000," he added, casually.

Marble floors? A herd of horses?

"No, just two horses," he said. "It's a high-tech barn with automatic watering troughs; things like that cost a lot."

The centerpiece of a Conrado house is a vineyard. "In high-end houses, having a vineyard is like having a Mercedes in the driveway," he said. "You look out of your window at your vines while you drink wine from your own backyard."

We pulled up to a 9,000-square-foot Mediterranean style home he'd built on a lot at the edge of Palo Alto just before it lifts into the foothills. The owner walked me through the house, which had a 12-seat movie theater and 1,200-bottle wine cellar. In the backyard a custom-built stream tumbled down a series of rocks to end in a pond, home to koi and a turtle—a nice vista for the guesthouse, which had a wood beam ceiling and its own kitchen.

As we pulled out of the driveway, the conversation drifted to the subject of big money and bigger money. Conrado mentioned one client worth 500 million dollars. "I can understand what 5 million dollars is," Conrado said. "I have a hard time understanding 500 million dollars. Of course, now that his options have dropped in value, he's only worth 30 million."

Had he been envious?

"It took me a long time not to go home and say: What's my problem? How come I didn't rise to that level? Then I realized money can't buy your way out of most of life's miseries. In this area your home is very important to you. That is probably why we build so many homes that feel like stages. People want to make a statement; their home is how they do it."

Melita Singh would be happy if she could find a home, any home, to rent, but for now she, her husband, and their three children will have to get by in a room in the Boccardo Reception Center, a shelter for the homeless in San Jose.

The Singhs are not poor. Mrs. Singh, who grew up in Trinidad, is a registered nurse who works in a nursing home. Mr. Singh works on contract for Hewlett-Packard. Between them, they have an income of $105,000.

But $105,000 a year isn't house-buying money in Silicon Valley, and the Singhs have the black mark of an eviction notice against them because of their noisy children. "You can throw money after scarce apartments all you want, but with an eviction you're not getting anything," said Maury Kendall of the Emergency Housing Consortium. So the Singhs are part of a new trend in homelessness. "It's no longer hobos and bums. It's working people— moms and dads impacted by the economic boom."

It is also a quirk of geography compounded by economics. The math is simple. The median apartment rental price is $1,600. There is a 5 percent vacancy rate in Silicon Valley.

> I can understand what 5 million dollars is. I have a hard time understanding 500 million dollars.

Rentals are at a premium; landlords rule.

"Why should a landlord have to contend with pets or kids when there are plenty of renters without such liabilities?" Kendall asked rhetorically. "We are reaping the harvest of years of poor planning. There is no affordable housing because it doesn't exist."

Yet, there was optimism from Mrs. Singh. "I see this as the land of opportunity," she effused, showing me their small room with pale yellow walls, tired gray carpet, and two double beds. She was feeding the baby, while three-year-old Josiah tugged at her shirt and five-year-old John bounced on the bed.

"I tell you why I came to America," she said. "In my country it's so limited. I love America. Land of opportunity. All will work out." She lay back on the bed and laughed.

Some don't even have the luxury of a heated room with access to a bath. "We have clients who come through the door who live in garages," Toni Wallace said. "They pay $500 to $600 a month for a garage with no toilet. Sometimes the space isn't insulated, let alone heated." Wallace is director of a social services center in East Palo Alto, the predominantly Hispanic and African-American city separated by a highway from its more affluent neighbor, Palo Alto.

Were things getting better?

"No," she replied. As electric bills soared, things were getting worse.

"It used to be you could go home at the end of the day and feel you helped someone. Now you just don't know," Wallace said.

"What do you do then?" I asked.

"We fall down, and we get back up."

The dot-com market had been in free fall, and at 550 Montgomery Street in San Francisco's financial district you could pick

With toys and computers battling for space in Dave Shelley and Laura Bowen's San Jose home, the line between producing computer games and raising two sons fades quickly. As Shelley lifts two-year-old Niall, the workstation becomes a playstation. Shelley finds comfort in Niall's visits: "It's refreshing to blow bubbles with him." Trendiness is not a distraction for Niall's mother. "We're out of the loop for Internet launch parties, BMWs, and designer clothes," says Bowen. "We think of the area as home rather than a hot spot."

through two floors of computer equipment and office furnishings from a defunct company called Stockpower.com to be auctioned the next day. Lee Harris, a businessman, looked at computers. He'd bought desks and cabinets at previous auctions, where, for example, a $60,000 server had sold for $5,000. "The buyers were jumping up and down," he said. "It's top quality stuff. Herman Miller chairs and office partitions that they practically pay you to take away." His eyes lit up. "There's a Mac!" he said, and left to inspect lot #1143 Apple Power Mac G3 with 4GB HDD.

Another dot-com ship had sunk. The flotsam and jetsam would go to the highest bidder. By late summer the *Industry Standard*, a magazine covering the Internet world, listed 139,643 dot-com layoffs since December 1999, then went belly-up itself.

What went wrong? "A lot of start-up companies should never have been funded," Karae Lisle said. She's a business consultant in Menlo Park and den mother to a support group for CEOs of companies in trouble. "The venture capitalists threw money at companies like they were slot machines. Pets.com? Like you're going to shove a 30-pound bag of dog food through the mail slot to me? What were they thinking?"

Standard business principles evaporated. "Every one of these kids was right out of business school," Lisle continued. "If someone gave you a pair of cleats, a bat, and a glove, and you only played catch with your dad and never dropped a ball, what makes you think you can play the World Series?"

"Do you know, Dave, your company is valued at 20 times Goodyear?" Curtis Heinz, a San Francisco stock trader, told a friend whose dot-com had skyrocketed.

"So who needs tires?" his friend replied.

Reports of the demise of Silicon Valley were premature. The patient wasn't moribund, merely temporarily indisposed.

"Every time Silicon Valley goes through a cycle, people say it's doomed," said AnnaLee Saxenian, a Berkeley professor of regional planning. "In 1980 I myself argued that housing and labor were too expensive, roads too crowded, that growth would shift elsewhere. Later they said it again, with the rise of technological Japan. But there are real companies here. It would be hard to argue that the Internet won't be an arena for business. It's a question of who survives. Silicon Valley is not the traditional model. There are social intangibles. It's not just dollars and cents."

In Silicon Valley the bust was not failure; it was part of the learning curve. "It's okay to fail nobly," explained Tom Melcher, who is in the middle of a start-up. "It's one of the bedrock things that make this place different. In the East, if you fail, you're a pariah. Not here."

Melcher's company, called There, involves the creation of an elaborate, sophisticated cyberspace playground, and it is, he knows, very high risk.

Lee Hwang left a well-paying job in Atlanta because she wanted a change. She found it at There. Her brother-in-law is the chief technology officer for the company, and she had been hired to keep Cokes in the refrigerator and answer the phone. "I sold off everything I had and came here to work a 12-hour day," she said, as we sat in the kitchen of the warehouse building that houses There in Menlo Park. "I have friends in Atlanta who think I'm

Silicon Valley sits on the edge of the future. Perhaps it even is the future. Yet, so many were being left behind.

crazy. Even if it tanks, it's an adventure. The coolness factor is high. I don't want to reach the end of my life and have any regrets."

Hwang, at least, could live with her sister and brother-in-law. At the building where There is taking shape, a handful of employees were living in their offices and sleeping on futons. "It's weird rolling out of bed and going to work," confessed Matt Murakami, a 24-year-old artist.

Murakami had moved from Orange County and, after a month's stay with relatives, decided to move into his cubicle. He was working late nights, anyway, and couldn't see paying $1,500 a month in rent. "I've put my life on hold till the IPO [initial public offering]," he said. "If it weren't for the skylight in the building, I wouldn't know if it was night or day."

One morning the newspaper carries a story about a partner at a venture capital firm. She has two cell phones—a Nokia 6100 and a Nokia 8860—and two handheld computers—a Palm Vx and a Handspring Visor Edge—not to mention a BlackBerry RIM 957 e-mail device. At home the lineup is three computers (one in the kitchen), four printers, and a fax. "The only time when I turn everything off is on a plane. Some may think that this is a character flaw, but I prefer to be 'always connected,'" she is quoted as saying.

Wired, perhaps. But connected?

The genius of Silicon Valley helped wire the world. Its enterprise could get you an airline ticket, a refrigerator, or stock quote at the click of a mouse. But the social fabric seemed to be unraveling. Though the Valley's per capita income increased 36 percent during the 1990s (the national increase was 17 percent), by the year 2000 a household at the bottom 20 percent of the distribution scale had less income than in 1993. The rising tide hadn't lifted all boats.

"We're like a specialized athlete. We just do innovation and invention," Jim Koch explains. Koch is director of the Center for Science, Technology and Society at Santa Clara University. He spoke about his recent report that examined the social capital—the community connectedness—of 40 different communities across the U.S. Although Silicon Valley ranked high in interracial trust and diversity of friendships, it landed near the bottom in civic engagement, charitable giving, volunteering, and civic leadership—and in sense of community as well.

There are reasons for this, Koch explained, and they have to do, in part, with a business ethos that eschews commitment. "The culture says you don't stay in one place very long. You jump from job to job.

"I think we feel lonelier and more isolated," he said. "I think life as a free agent is not what it's cracked up to be."

Chinese New Year was approaching, and at the Lion Plaza mall on Tully Road—one of those faux California-mission confections of aqua and terra-cotta concrete—you could find Johnny Au selling plants. "For good fortune," Au said, explaining the tradition. "Buy these pussy willows for silver," he pulled a branch from a bucket. "And this tree," he indicated a 15-year-old bonsai with yellow flowers, "for gold."

A New Year in all cultures is a chance to look back to the past and ahead to the future.

Silicon Valley could look back to a wild ride in which start-ups flared and fizzled. But Silicon Valley prefers to look forward. The Valley is about ideas and invention, but it is also about money—which happens to be one of the things people wish for you on the Chinese New Year.

I had driven to Redwood City, the not-quite-as-chic town north of Atherton, to talk to George J. Leonard, a professor of humanities and Asian studies at San Francisco State University. We sat in his teahouse, a sanctuary really, in back of his modest home while Leonard poured green tea into thimble-like cups. As the fragrance of tea filled the room, we admired the translucent glaze of a celadon bowl and an earthenware pot in the shape of a lotus leaf. Silicon Valley sits on the edge of the future. Perhaps it even is the future. Yet, so many were being left behind. The contrasts were as unsettling as the earthquake zone that helps define its geography. To keep my balance, I needed an anchor, a steady handhold. Leonard offered one, using as a framework the teachings of Confucius.

"Confucius says, 'Of course, you want to be rich and famous,'" Leonard said. "'It's natural. Wealth and fame are what every man desires.'" But Confucius understood there is a moral decision too, and sooner or later an accounting begins.

"'The question,' Confucius said, 'is what are you willing to trade for it?'"

Discussion Questions

- How does the earthquake that opens the article reverberate throughout? Consider both actual and metaphorical "aftershocks."

- What is "techno-optimism"? Does it persist in the United States? What about elsewhere in the world?

- What does one gain from being constantly connected by cell phone, Facebook, and other social media? What does one lose?

- What are working conditions like in Silicon Valley's high-tech world? To what extent have they come to characterize workplaces and ideas of work elsewhere?

Writing Activities

- In what ways does Silicon Valley demonstrate "'a business ethos that eschews commitment'"? What are some of the consequences, not only for the high-tech industry, but also for society?

- Examine the idea and the reality of home and homelessness in Silicon Valley, as portrayed in this article. "Rootlessness" could be a related topic to pursue, as well.

- Compare the idea of "connectivity" with that of "community," and, in the process, reflect on your own social networking practices as well.

- What version of the "American Dream" is obtained in Silicon Valley? As you consider the question, compare other versions that are represented in this reader (in "Changing America," "How Walt Disney Changed Everything," and elsewhere).

Collaborative Activities

- Do you think that anyone who can afford multi-million dollar houses with vineyards and stables has a justifiable right to build them? If that's one way an individual can fulfill his or her dream, how does doing so affect others who are not as fortunate? In debating this question, consider such practicalities as access to health care and education not only about Silicon Valley, but also other areas in the country.

- Given that this article was written over a decade ago, are some of the issues it raised outdated? What about those that are still current? And how do they resonate in your world? In the process of thinking about these questions, focus also on the language of Silicon Valley and the extent to which it has permeated and even become native your world.

NEW ORLEANS: A PERILOUS FUTURE

Protected only by dwindling wetlands and flawed levees, New Orleans is sinking further below rising seas and facing stronger hurricanes. Some experts say that the question isn't whether another disaster on the scale of Hurricane Katrina will hit New Orleans, but when. Even so, people are returning to the city they call home, and rebuilding yet again. At what cost?

As you read "New Orleans: A Perilous Future," you should consider the following questions:

- How would you feel if your home was devastated? Can you empathize with the residents of New Orleans?

- As you read the article below, keep the topic of insurance in mind, not only as a practical consideration but also as a concept, along with any questions that arise.

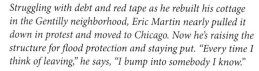

Struggling with debt and red tape as he rebuilt his cottage in the Gentilly neighborhood, Eric Martin nearly pulled it down in protest and moved to Chicago. Now he's raising the structure for flood protection and staying put. "Every time I think of leaving," he says, "I bump into somebody I know."

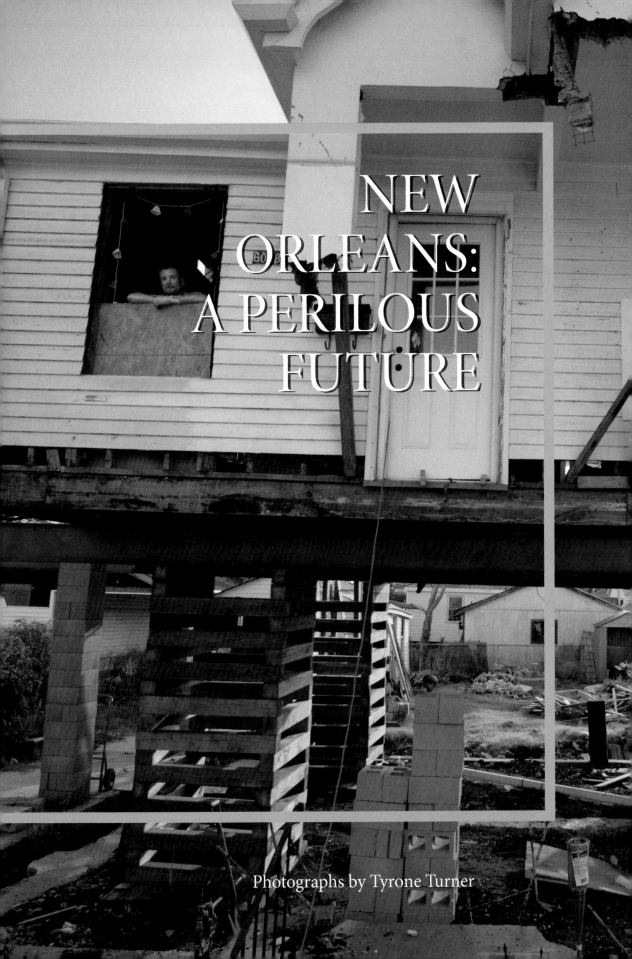

NEW ORLEANS: A PERILOUS FUTURE

Photographs by Tyrone Turner

With a slide and a shuffle, the Big Nine Social Aid and Pleasure Club parades past empty houses on Forstall Street in the Lower Ninth Ward. The city's deep-rooted culture draws many back home despite the risks. "I've been in two major floods in 40 years," says club president Ronald Lewis (not shown). "That's pretty good odds. I hope we have another 40 years to live our life to the fullest."

BORN AMID WILLOW AND CYPRESS SWAMPS ATOP SQUISHY DELTA SOILS, DIE-HARD RESIDENTS
REFUSE TO GIVE UP
ON THE CRESCENT CITY, NEW ORLEANS, LA.

Hurricane Katrina, the costliest natural disaster in United States history, was also a warning shot. Right after the tragedy, many people expressed a defiant resolve to rebuild the city. But among engineers and experts, that resolve is giving way to a growing awareness that another such disaster is inevitable, and nothing short of a massive and endless national commitment can prevent it.

Located in one of the lowest spots in the United States, the Big Easy is already as much as 17 feet below sea level in places, and it continues to sink, by up to an inch a year. Upstream dams and levees built to tame Mississippi River floods and ease shipping have starved the delta downstream of sediments and nutrients, causing wetlands that once buffered the city against storm-driven seas to sink beneath the waves. Louisiana has lost 1,900 square miles of coastal lands since the 1930s; Katrina and Hurricane Rita together took out 217 square miles, putting the city that much closer to the open Gulf. Most ominous of all, global warming is raising the Gulf faster than at any time since the last ice age thawed. Sea level could rise several feet over the next century. Even before then, hurricanes may draw ever more energy from warming seas and grow stronger and more frequent.

And the city's defenses are down. Despite having spent a billion dollars already, the U.S. Army Corps of Engineers now estimates it will take until after 2010 to strengthen the levee system enough to withstand a 1-in-100-year storm, roughly the size of Category 3 Katrina. It would take decades more to protect the Big Easy from the truly Big One, a Category 4 or 5—if engineers can agree on how to do that and if Congress agrees to foot the almost unimaginable bill. For now, even a modest, Category 2 storm could reflood the city.

> **L**ocated in one of the lowest spots in the United States, the Big Easy is already as much as 17 feet below sea level in some places, and it continues to sink, by up to an inch per year.

Adapted from "New Orleans: A Perilous Future" by Joel L. Bourne, Jr.: National Geographic Magazine, August 2007.

The long odds led Robert Giegengack, a geologist at the University of Pennsylvania, to tell policymakers a few months after the storm that the wealthiest, most technologically advanced nation on the globe was helpless to prevent another Katrina: "We simply lack the capacity to protect New Orleans." He recommended selling the French Quarter to Disney, moving the port 150 miles upstream, and abandoning one of the most historic and culturally significant cities in the nation. Others have suggested rebuilding it as a smaller, safer enclave on higher ground.

But history, politics, and love of home are powerful forces in the old river town. Instead of rebuilding smarter or surrendering, New Orleans is doing what it has always done after such disasters: bumping up the levees just a little higher, rebuilding the same flood-prone houses back in the same low spots, and praying that hurricanes hit elsewhere. Some former New Orleanians may have had enough. More than a third of the city's pre-Katrina population has yet to return. Those who have face deserted neighborhoods, surging crime, skyrocketing insurance, and a tangle of red tape—simply to rebuild in harm's way.

If Paris, as Hemingway said, is a movable feast, then New Orleans has always been a floating one. Born amid willow and cypress swamps atop squishy delta soils, the city originally perched on the high ground formed by over-wash deposits from annual river floods. Jean-Baptiste Le Moyne, Sieur de Bienville, actually had to wait for the water to recede before he could plant the French flag in 1718. A flood destroyed the village the year after he founded it, and hurricanes wiped it off the map in 1722 and again a year later. In its

We simply lack the capacity to protect New Orleans.

289-year history, major hurricanes or river floods have put the city under 27 times, about once every 11 years. Each time, the fractious French, Spanish, blacks, Creoles, and Cajuns raised the levees and rebuilt.

Until the 20th century, they kept to the high ground along the Mississippi River and on three nearby rises—the Metairie, Gentilly, and Espla-nade Ridges. But in the early 1900s a brilliant city engineer, A. Baldwin Wood, invented massive pumps, up to 14 feet in diameter, that were used to drain the great cypress "backswamp." The booming metropolis began spilling north toward Lake Pontchartrain. As the swamp soils dried, they shrank and compacted, slumping below sea level. In every flood since, the newer, lower neighborhoods suffered the most as the waters found their former haunts in the old swamp.

The great tragedy of Katrina is that the hard lessons learned in those earlier storms were blithely forgotten by all. After the great Mississippi River flood of 1927 wreaked havoc all along its course and came within a few feet of spilling over the river levees and inundating New Orleans, the growing city clamored for additional protection. Over the coming decades, the federal government erected a vast network of levees and spillways along the river and around the city, while giant new dams along the Missouri—the Mississippi's longest tributary—ponded water all the way to South Dakota. The system was billed as a triumph of engineering over nature.

Yet Gilbert F. White, considered the "father of floodplain management," came to a far different conclusion, one that Katrina drove home with a vengeance. As a young University of Chicago geographer, White had studied the delta after the 1927 disaster and realized that much of the suffering

Louisiana is losing roughly 12 square miles of storm-buffering wetlands each year as levees block sediment, canals are dredged, and ground subsides. In 2005 Hurricanes Katrina and Rita took out 217 square miles, much of it east and south of New Orleans. Some areas scoured by Katrina may never recover.

could have been avoided. "Floods are 'acts of God,'" he wrote in 1942, "but flood losses are largely acts of man." White and his colleagues argued that dams, levees, and other flood protections may actually increase flood losses because they spur new development in the floodplain, which incurs catastrophic losses when man-made flood protections fail. The phenomenon came to be known as the "levee effect."

After Katrina taller, stronger floodwalls now glisten in the breaches, their clean white concrete contrasting starkly with the still ruined neighborhoods behind them, while massive new black floodgates are poised to close the canals at the lakefront. The rebuilt hurricane protection system gives returning New Orleanians some sense of security. But the corps has yet to fix what many see as the weakest link in the system, the 76-mile ship channel called the Mississippi River Gulf Outlet—Mr. Go to the locals—which the corps dug east of town in the late 1950s and early 1960s.

On a steamy summer afternoon with squalls in the offing, coastal scientists Paul Kemp of Louisiana State University and John Lopez of the Lake Pontchartrain Basin Foundation set out by boat to inspect the "funnel," formed east of town by the levees lining the MRGO and another channel that converges with it, the Gulf Intracoastal Waterway. Computer models run by Kemp's colleagues at LSU show the funnel raised Katrina's massive surge by more than three feet in the Industrial Canal, overtopping and destroying floodwalls protecting the Lower Ninth Ward. Farther east, the storm surge hammered through more than eight miles of the MRGO levees, which in turn wiped out much of St. Bernard Parish.

St. Bernard residents had been clamoring for years for the corps to close the little-used channel they call the "hurricane highway." Touted as a shortcut to the port for ocean freighters, the channel instead destroyed tens of thousands of acres of wetlands. It brought in salt water that killed marsh plants, while the wakes of the few ships eroded the banks of the channel, widening it from 500 feet to almost a half mile in places. One lesson of Katrina is simple, says Lopez: Close MRGO.

The corps says it now intends to do so. But when or how the channel might be shut down is anyone's guess. Congress has yet to give a green light. "If we don't close MRGO," says Lopez, "it might be time to do what my wife says and move to Kansas."

Though the corps denies that the channel amplified Katrina's surge, everyone agrees that its levees—St. Bernard's primary hurricane defense—failed miserably. The corps insists the structures simply weren't high enough to withstand Katrina's 17 feet of surge and six-foot waves. But at many of the breaches, the levees were built of weak sand and shell dredged from the canal itself. Kemp believes the shell-sand sections began to collapse as soon as the waves started breaking on them, long before the main surge hit. He also notes that where these levees were fronted by intact wetlands or trees, they survived. Where they ended directly in the water, they failed.

Old ways die hard in the bayou. Even after the dramatic failure of the shell sand in the levees, independent investigators found corps contractors using the same material to rebuild them. Only after the discovery was made public did the corps barge in yellowish clay from Mississippi to cap the levees. And

> The frequency of truly monster storms—Categories 4 and 5—have doubled since 1970.

parts of the new structures still have no buffer against erosion.

Kemp points to a new section of bare levee right next to the channel and shakes his head. "This is a recipe for disaster," he mutters. "The waves are going to break right on that thing. If a big storm comes in here this year, it's gone." Even sections of the levees newly capped with clay are already eroding from rainfall, Kemp says. In fact, during a recent inspection, engineering professor Bob Bea, who helped lead the UC Berkeley team that investigated the levee failures, found multiple chinks in the city's hurricane armor, from newly eroded levees along MRGO to Katrina-battered floodwalls that had not been repaired.

"When you start thinking about long-term protection, it doesn't give me any confidence," says Bea, a former resident of New Orleans who actually lost his home during Hurricane Betsy. "The system is ratty, shot full of defects. My advice for the people in low-lying areas: I wouldn't start rebuilding my life there."

Yet many are doing just that, regardless of what the experts say, with a typical New Orleans cocktail of denial, faith in the levees, and 100-proof love of home. Three months after the storm, when much of the city still lay in ruins, the mere suggestion by a blue-ribbon panel of planners from the Urban Land Institute to hold off rebuilding the lowest areas set off a howl of protests. Mayor C. Ray Nagin, who was in a tight election race at the time, dropped the notion of "shrinking the footprint" like a hot beignet, as did his opponent, Lieutenant Governor Mitch Landrieu. The mayor, however, fell short of promising every neighborhood city services.

"We are going to come back, and we want the world to know it," says Lanier Hosford. "It's one of the most magical cities in the world," Hosford says. But is the magic strong enough to save it? "Absolutely, positively, yes, without a doubt."

To make matters even more confusing, the federal government declared it would offer flood insurance for most new or substantially rebuilt houses only if they were raised by several feet. Yet the city government granted exemptions to many returning homeowners, grandfathering their houses at their prior elevations. The result has been an unplanned patchwork recovery, with some people raising their homes to protect against floods and others building right back where they were in the lowest sections of the city.

Keysha Finley didn't wait for the levees to be fixed. Just nine months before the storm, Finley had moved into a new four-bedroom brick house off Bullard Avenue, in one of the tonier neighborhoods of New Orleans East. Singer Aaron Neville lived in the posh Eastover subdivision nearby. Though most media attention has focused on the working-class Lower Ninth Ward, the damage was just as bad in New Orleans East, a bastion of middle- and upper-class black flight from crime and failing schools in the inner city. It's also one of the lowest sections of the city, with some areas more than ten feet below sea level.

Less than a year after the flood, Finley was back. Her kitchen, where four feet of muddy water sloshed for weeks, is now filled with warm Mediterranean colors and has a new tile floor. Is she concerned about the low elevation? "It was never a consideration," she says. "Before we bought, we asked the neighbors if it ever flooded. They said never."

Nearby houses remained boarded up and empty for months, but now the neighbors are rebuilding, reassuring Finley that she and her husband were right to return. "I know things happen wherever you go. You can't run from them," she says. But the months of stress have taken their toll. "If it happens again, I won't come back. I don't think I could go through this again."

The die-hard refusal to give up on home persists in the Lower Ninth Ward, where many houses had been in families for decades. Caught by a pincer of tidal waves coming from the blown-out levees to the east and the blown-out floodwalls of the Industrial Canal to the west, the black working-class neighborhood stewed in floodwaters for four weeks. Residents were not allowed to move back for another two months, to the utter dismay of Tanya Harris, an organizer for the community-rights group ACORN. Harris's family had lived for 60 years in the hardest hit section, north of Claiborne Avenue, what she calls "way back-a-town."

"My neighborhood was an extension of the inside of my house," she says, driving over the rusty drawbridge over the Industrial Canal. "When I turned off Claiborne Avenue after work, it would take me 20 minutes to drive the last ten blocks home because I've got to wave to Aunt May and 20 other people. I'd complain about it, but I loved it."

Aunt May left after the storm, as did the kids who once played in the streets. The last ten blocks to Harris's home remain the same blur of destruction that blazed over television screens across the nation, with most houses abandoned or destroyed. Her house survived, a one-story yellow brick affair with red shutters. Twenty months after the storm, her renovations were nearly complete, and she hoped to move in soon.

The tortoise pace of repairing fractured sewer and water lines in the Lower Ninth originally fed suspicions that the city would take the Urban Land Institute's advice and redevelop the neighborhood with higher income homes and condos near the river

and green space way back-a-town, replacing the derelict houses. But thanks largely to the efforts of Harris and ACORN, the city in March included the Lower Ninth in its rebuilding plan, which provides seed money for redevelopment. In fact, one of the first two new houses built in the neighborhood belongs to Harris's grandmother, Josephine Butler, the five-foot-tall, 85-year-old matriarch of her clan. "Nobody," says Harris, "not Ray Nagin, not George Bush, is going to tell her what to do."

The reality remains daunting for those trying to rebuild, or trying to decide whether to come back at all. The risk of catastrophic flooding is rising year by year, with no end in sight—in no small part because the city is sinking.

Even before it was covered by millions of tons of floodwater, New Orleans had sunk well below sea level, because of the draining and compacting of the backswamp and the pumping of groundwater. According to the latest satellite measurements, the city continues to sink at around two-tenths of an inch each year. The rate is faster in Lakeview and fastest of all in neighborhoods to the east and west. In St. Bernard Parish, subsidence tops out at nearly an inch a year. Some sections of the MRGO levees have sunk up to four feet since they were built, according to Roy Dokka, an LSU geologist who co-authored the satellite study, and Katrina breached many of the low spots.

"This is a place where people shouldn't be living, yet we're here," says Dokka. "But subsidence isn't going to kill people. It's the ever increasing vulnerability to storm surges and our inability to prepare for them."

Sinking is only part of the city's elevation challenge. Over the thousands of years when the delta beneath the city was being formed, sea level was almost stable. But as climate change warms the oceans and melts glaciers, sea level is rising by three millimeters a year. In February a United Nations panel on climate change predicted that seas would be more than a foot higher by 2100. And one of the nation's top climate scientists thinks that forecast is far too modest. James Hansen, director of the NASA Goddard Institute for Space Studies in New York City, notes new data from satellites showing accelerated melting of the vast ice sheets in Greenland and West Antarctica. "If we go down the business-as-usual path," he says, "we will get sea level rise measured in meters this century."

The impact on New Orleans? A meter of sea level rise would be enough to turn New Orleans into the new Big Easy Reef—or a new Amsterdam, behind massive dikes. That's assuming that big hurricanes don't come more often; chances are they will. Hurricane frequency in the Atlantic waxes and wanes over a decades-long cycle that is now on the upswing. For this year, hurricane forecasters are predicting seven to ten hurricanes in the Atlantic Basin, with up to five reaching Category 3 or above—more than double the average from 1950 to 2000. The Gulf Coast faces 50-50 odds of being hit by a Katrina-size storm this summer. Already, tropical storms in the Atlantic are 50 percent more common than at the previous peak, in the 1950s, say Peter Webster and Judith Curry of the Georgia Institute of Technology. The frequency of truly monster storms—Categories 4 and 5—has doubled since 1970.

These trends have persuaded some researchers that the natural cycle is not the only factor driving up hurricane activity. Global warming is boosting sea-surface temperatures in hurricane alley—the tropical Atlantic and Caribbean—and warm seas are rocket fuel for stronger hurricanes. Before

> There are people who will fight to the death to stay here because it's such a damned joy to live here.

Katrina made landfall, it had exploded from a Category 3 storm to a Category 5 in 12 hours, partly because it stirred up a deep pocket of warm water in the Gulf. Only when it reached the Louisiana coast did the storm weaken again to a Category 3, sparing New Orleans an even greater catastrophe. If global warming produces stronger storms on top of the decadal cycle, 2005, with Katrina, Rita, and two other mega-hurricanes in the Atlantic, could be a stormy precursor of the coming century.

But even if wind and water give the Big Easy a respite until the corps can guarantee legitimate 1-in-100-year hurricane protection, powerful social and demographic forces unleashed by Katrina may already be undermining the city's revival. Researchers have found that major disasters tend to accelerate existing social and economic trends. A booming San Francisco rebuilt bigger and better after its 1906 earthquake and fire; while the decaying industrial city of Tangshan, China, needed a huge infusion of aid from the government to recover after a giant earthquake in 1976—and was ultimately saved by the country's burgeoning economy. It's a sobering precedent for New Orleans, which has been plagued for decades by economic decline—just a single *Fortune* 500 company is still headquartered there—shrinking population, failing schools, and high crime.

"So why protect it? Why protect a piece of history that's a cross between Williamsburg and Sodom and Gomorrah?" Oliver Houck, a Tulane professor of environmental law, sat in his office, hands locked behind his head, pondering the question on everyone's mind. "There are people who will fight to the death to stay here because it's such a damned joy to live here."

After she gutted two flood-damaged rooms of her childhood home in the Lower Ninth Ward, the memories got too strong for Nikkisha Neapollioun, so her son sat down to console her. Though she loves New Orleans, she has little confidence in the levees or the elected leaders. "It's like placing a Band-Aid on open-heart surgery and then saying come on back, it's OK!"

But at what price? Houck paused for a moment to gaze out his window at the oak-strewn Tulane campus. The university lost two departments and a quarter of its students to Katrina, while he and his family spent months in exile after the storm. "If two words characterize all of southern Louisiana now, they would be 'total uncertainty,'" Houck says. "It's the total talk around the table. It's the conversation you're having with friends and spouses, even strangers. What do we do now?"

Discussion Questions

- Does it take a particular kind of person to live in New Orleans?

- What are some of the social and emotional costs associated with Katrina in New Orleans? What about beyond the city itself?

- In 1942, Gilbert F. White, the so-called "father of flood-plain management," wrote: "Floods are 'acts of God,' but flood losses are largely acts of man." How does Joel K. Bourne develop the point in this article? Does the observation hold true even after many decades have passed and significant technological and engineering advances have been made?

- While New Orleans has been repeatedly devastated by floods, it's hardly the only disaster-prone city in the nation. Think of San Francisco and the San Andreas Fault. Why take the chance of building and rebuilding in such places, over and over?

Writing Activities

- Given the information provided in this article, do you think the areas of New Orleans decimated by Katrina should be rebuilt or abandoned?

- In the best of all possible worlds, could science and engineering provide security against natural disasters? Is it hubris to imagine that humans could anticipate catastrophes and offset their effects?

- Like many other selections in this reader, this article examines the relationship between place and identity. What, in your case, does where you come from have to do with who you are?

- "'If two words characterize all of southern Louisiana now,' observes a professor whom Bourne quotes at the end of the article, they would be 'total uncertainty.... It's the total talk you're having around the table. It's the conversation you're having with friends and spouses, even strangers. What do we do now?" Faced with such uncertainty, how would you reply to the question yourself? Does it resonate beyond New Orleans in some ways, perhaps even to the human condition itself?

Collaborative Activities

- Do you think taxpayers should bear the burden of disaster relief? As you debate the issue, consider also whether taxpayers should bear the burden of rebuilding in areas known to be prone to natural disasters.

- Research other famous floating cities, such as Venice and Amsterdam, and compare their histories with that of New Orleans.

ZipUSA: FARGO, ND 58102; THE FARGO THAT WASN'T IN THE MOVIE

Of the 275 U.S. cities ranked by size, Fargo, North Dakota, is down near the bottom of the list, at #254. At the same time, the critical acclaim and popularity of the 1996 movie *Fargo* gave the city a prominent place on the American cultural map. As David Beers reflects on the film version, he also provides insight into what makes the real Fargo tick.

As you read "The Fargo that Wasn't in the Movie," you should consider the following question:

- As you read this article, do you find that it matters whether you've seen the film version of *Fargo* or not?

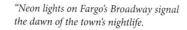

"Neon lights on Fargo's Broadway signal the dawn of the town's nightlife.

ZipUSA: FARGO, NORTH DAKOTA 58102; THE FARGO THAT WASN'T IN THE MOVIE

Photographs by Nina Berman

Facing minus 10°F, Meredith Meyer trudges to work in a homemade snorkel hood—as quirky as the Oscar-winning film that made her town famous. People look twice, she says, but only out of jealousy. In Fargo, ingenuity is as plentiful as snow.

INCREDIBLY RESILIENT FOLKS
OF FARGO, NORTH DAKOTA.

Tami Smith has already made history. She's the first woman ever to head up the annual Kiwanis Club Pancake Karnival in Fargo, North Dakota. Now she's hoping the 45th Karnival will break all records. To do so would mean feeding breakfast to 11,000 people on a single Saturday in February, a feat approachable only if Smith's dozens of volunteers flip, fry, serve, and swipe clean with crack precision.

The charity event is such a Fargo tradition that it's a coveted civic honor to be anointed a pancake flipper. (When one Karnival stalwart died, his wife requested that pancakes be flipped at his funeral. And so they were.)

Smith and her team attend to the final details at the Fargo Civic Center the day before the Karnival. Ten thousand cartons of milk. Check. Twelve thousand plastic bottles of syrup. Check. Griddle number two, a round one that rotates, is down, but Dave Duff, product manager for a local tractor company, is sure he can fix the broken bearing. Jerry Hartford, a mechanical engineer, unfolds his new blueprint for efficiently routing long lines of the hungry.

But what you don't remember is Fargo itself, for not a frame was shot here.

Eleven thousand cartons of orange juice. Check.

Seven years ago Smith, who is 31 and sells promotional products, was dismayed to learn her employer was transferring her to Fargo. "I told them if they didn't move me again in six months, I'd quit." She flashes a smile, resting busy hands for a moment on her fulsomely pregnant stomach. "I soon found myself loving it here."

It is no small thing to profess one's love of Fargo in the dead of winter. Even in November there are days when it is colder here than at the North Pole, days when snow might not fall but prairie winds whip up snow already on the ground (and a fair amount of dirt) to cause a blinding horizontal blizzard.

If you saw the movie *Fargo,* you remember the impossibly flat whiteness. But what you don't remember is Fargo itself, for not a frame was shot here. And so you may not know that Fargo is a city of 91,000 people with another 33,000 just across the Red River in Moorhead,

Adapted from "ZipUSA: Fargo, North Dakota 58102, The Fargo that Wasn't in the Movie" by David Beers: National Geographic Magazine, November 2003.

Robust winter winds sweep a sideways blizzard across the plains. Weeks after doing some sweeping of her own, Ruth Urang suffered a stroke. Says Ruth, who doesn't smoke or drink: "So much for clean living."

at the Fargo Theatre. The national news media arrived to get in on the joke. But Margie Bailly, who runs the 1926 art deco theater, had the last laugh. Drawing all that attention to her faded gem of a movie palace attracted more funding to restore it.

Weeks later, as a particularly nasty winter melted into a flood, the news media was back. With friendly tenacity and no showing off, Fargoans filled and set 3.5 million sandbags to defy the swollen Red River. Dennis Walaker, the bear-size director of Fargo Public Works, emerged as a local hero.

Fargoans do not coddle their heroes. When 80-year-old Ruth Urang catches sight of Walaker on the street, she lets him have it: "Tell your road crews to stop tossing these economy-size hunks of ice on my walk." Only after Walaker promises, and is out of earshot, does Urang say, "He saved the city. If it weren't for him, we'd all be nine feet under."

Urang, who has just returned from a friend's funeral, is attacking the snow in front of her crisply modest home with a fresh yellow-bristled broom. She wears a light coat and skirt. Her shins are bared to the 20-below windchill.

No, you don't let a little threat of frostbite cramp your style in Fargo. So on an average way-below-zero morning, you may spy Ronald Davenport cycling to his bank job, his face mask collecting a crust of ice crystals. At noon bundled-up Matt Halverson casually barbecues bratwurst outside Metro Drug at Second and Broadway. After dinner Hannah Berg, 7, braves the icy wind to arrive at Horace Mann Elementary School's outdoor rink. The other kids, all older, blindfold her so she can kneel on the ice and sort their hockey sticks to decide teams for a pickup game. And in the coldest late hours, two nearly naked souls stand on a fire escape, steam billowing off them. They have just emerged from the sauna at the Spirit Room gallery and yoga studio. They place blocks of wood under their feet to keep from sticking to the freezing metal.

On the morning of the Pancake Karnival, the griddle action is intense. "My eyelashes are melted together," says LeAnn Koehler, a

Minnesota. Or that freight trains rumble and moan through the low-slung downtown day and night. Or that within one zip code, 58102, there is a medical center that broadcasts robotic surgeries, a historic Broadway being restored to former glory, and a library where young refugees from Bosnia, Sudan, and Somalia crowd around computer screens, catching up on news from home.

What *Fargo* did get right is the friendly tenacity of Fargoans, says Kristin Rudrüd, an actress who played the kidnapped wife in the film and who lives here with her ten-year-old daughter. "That spirit of pressing on, one foot in front of the other, with a good heart," is how Fargoans get through their winters, she says. "People seem to obey the Scandinavian concept of *janteloven*. It means, basically, 'Don't show off.'"

When *Fargo* captivated moviegoers with its "Ya! You betcha!" heartland stereotypes in 1996, Fargo responded with an ironic wink. Residents wore their goofiest ear-flapped caps for an Academy Awards gala held downtown first-time flipper. "Next time I won't wear mascara." Two griddles down Alex Sahr shares the wisdom of his 85 years. "When it gets dry around the edges, flip it. But don't flip it too high."

Right. Might be a violation of janteloven.

Tami Smith, wearing a headset to command her troops, takes a cell phone call from a fellow Kiwanian lying on a beach somewhere in the Caribbean. "The sausage fryer keeps blowing fuses," she tells him. "Otherwise, we're doing pretty good."

More janteloven, actually. Tami and her Karnival crew will break the record they care about most, raising more than $30,000 for charity, their highest amount ever, while serving a near record 10,737 attendees.

Out there among the breakfasting throng bobs a lonely Mohawk haircut of blue and yellow spikes. It belongs to Jake Boucher, 15, who, having downed his last flapjack, is eager to leave this Karnival for another carnival.

That would be the city's first Winter Carnival, featuring punk rock and homegrown avant-garde. Eighteen bands play for no pay at the Fargo Theatre. At one point local drag queens appear on stage to lip-synch tunes by Cher and other divas.

And just after midnight, at show's end, the mighty Wurlitzer pipe organ rises from its pit. The man at the four banks of keys is the furthest thing from the shrieking headbangers who just preceded him onstage. But silver-haired Dave Knudtson, employed here at the theater for more than a quarter century, pumps forth a melody from his youth, "Mister Sandman," that soothes and pleases the weary teenagers clustered around.

Statistics show North Dakota is having a difficult time keeping its young people in the state. But tonight, in Fargo at least, no one's in a hurry to leave the party.

Discussion Questions

- What kind of person does it take to live in Fargo? Why would anyone want to live there at all?

- According to Beers, Fargoans "seem to obey the Scandinavian concept of janteloven," which "means, basically, don't show off." How does this mesh, or not, with American character traits?

Writing Activities

- What does the annual Kiwanis Club Pancake Karnival say about the Fargoans? In addressing this question, do some further research on Kiwanis Clubs, as well.

- Describe the place you consider home. What are its main features? What about the people who live there? What are they like? How do environment and identity relate and interact?

Collaborative Activities

- As the article notes, several distinct immigrant populations have settled in Fargo over time. Dividing these up among study groups in the class, find out what you can about your respective immigrants, why they've come to United States, and why they've settled in Fargo. What does the city offer them? What do they offer in return?

TAKE IN THE STATE FAIR WITH GARRISON KEILLOR

"Roomsful of total strangers under mass hypnosis! The world's largest and most polite corndog chomp! Farm adolescents well versed in animal husbandry! Mothers who look like daughters and vice versa! Candy apples, pork chops on a stick, and fried Coca-Cola! Young men who want you to become a career beautician!" These are some the idiosyncratic and the typical features of the state fairs Keillor tours, as he makes sense of the enduring appeal of this old-fashioned institution.

As you read "Take in the State Fair With Garrison Keillor," consider the following questions:

- What is the author's tone in this essay? How is it related to the experience of a state fair?
- In the end, did you enjoy taking in the fair with Keillor? Would you want to go—in reality and/or in imagination—again?

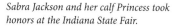

Sabra Jackson and her calf Princess took honors at the Indiana State Fair.

TAKE IN THE STATE FAIR WITH GARRISON KEILLOR

Photographs by Joel Sartore

Eating into history, 8,400 Iowa fairgoers bite in synchrony at the first-ever Corn Dog Chomp, in 2008. Recipes vary (bacon fat makes some extra tasty), but corn dogs have been fair fare since at least the 1940s. A new treat debuted in Texas in 2006: fried Coca-Cola (batter balls flavored with cola syrup).

THE STATE FAIR IS

A RITUAL CARNIVAL MARKING THE END OF SUMMER

AND GARDENS AND APPLE ORCHARDS AND THE START OF SCHOOL AND HIGHER ALGEBRA AND THE IMPOSITION OF STRICT RULES AND WHAT WE IN THE NORTH CALL THE LONG DARK TIME. LIKE GARDENING, THE FAIR DOESN'T CHANGE ALL THAT MUCH.

The big wheel whirls and the girls squeal and the bratwursts cook on the little steel rollers and the boys slouch around and keep checking their hair. It isn't the World's Columbian Exposition, the Aquarian Exposition, the Great Exhibition of the Works of Industry of All Nations, the Exposition Universelle, the Gathering of the Tribes, or the Aspen Institute. It's just us, taking a break from digging potatoes.

The Ten Chief Joys of the State Fair are:

1. To eat food with your two hands.

2. To feel extreme centrifugal force reshaping your face and jowls as you are flung or whirled turbulently and you experience that intense joyfulness that is indistinguishable from anguish, or (as you get older) to observe other persons in extreme centrifugal situations.

3. To mingle, merge, mill, jostle gently, and flock together with throngs, swarms, mobs, and multitudes of persons slight or hefty, punky or preppy, young or ancient, wandering through the hubbub and amplified razzmatazz and raw neon and clouds of wiener steam in search of some elusive thing, nobody is sure exactly what.

The Midwest is State Fair Central, and it thrives here because we are the breadbasket of America.

4. To witness the stupidity of others, their gluttony and low-grade obsessions, their poor manners and slack-jawed, mouth-breathing, pop-eyed yahootude, and feel rather sophisticated by comparison.

5. To see the art of salesmanship, of barking, hustling, touting, and see how effectively it works on others and not on cool you.

6. To see designer chickens, the largest swine, teams of mighty draft horses, llamas, rare breeds of geese, geckos, poisonous snakes, a two-headed calf, a 650-pound man, and whatever else appeals to the keen, inquiring mind.

7. To watch the judging of livestock.

8. To observe entertainers attempt to engage a crowd that is moving laterally.

9. To sit down and rest amid the turmoil and reconsider the meaning of life.

10. To turn away from food and amusement and crass pleasure and to resolve to live on a higher plane from now on.

Adapted from "Take in the State Fair with Garrison Keillor" by Garrison Keillor: National Geographic Magazine, July 2009.

The Midwest is State Fair Central, and it thrives here because we are the breadbasket of America, Hog Butcher, Machinemaker, Stacker of Particleboard, Player With Chain Saws, Land of the Big Haunches. And also because Midwesterners are insular, industrious, abstemious, introspective people skittish about body contact, and a state fair is liberation from all of that, a plunge into the pool of self-indulgence, starting with a thick pork chop hot off the grill and served on a stick with a band of crisp brown fat along one side. The fat is not good for you. You eat the pork chop, fat and all, and your child eats her pork chop, and then you score a giant vanilla shake from the Dairy Bar to cushion the fall of a bagful of tiny doughnuts. Now you're warmed up and ready to move on to the corn dog course.

But first here is a flume ride your child is agitating for, so you climb onto a steel raft and plunge into a concrete gorge and over a waterfall, and a two-foot wave washes over the gunwales, and now your pants are soaked. You disembark. You look like a man who could not contain his excitement. For cover, you hide in the crowd. You walk close behind people. You join the throng at the hot-corn stand and comfort yourself with a salty ear of buttered corn. Your pants chafe. You wander among booths of merchandise looking for men's pants and find encyclopedias, storm windows, lawn mowers, vegetable peelers and choppers, humidifiers, log splitters, and home saunas. Your search for dry pants leads you through buildings where champion jams and jellies are displayed on tables draped with purple, blue, red, yellow ribbons, and also champion cakes (angel food, Bundt light, Bundt dark, chiffon, chocolate, chocolate chiffon, German chocolate, jelly roll, pound, spice, sponge, vegetable, or fruit) and pickles (beet, bean, bread-and-butter, cucumber sweet, dill without garlic, dill with garlic, peppers sweet,

Farming is about work and about there being a Right Way and a Wrong Way to do it.

peppers hot, watermelon). And through an education pavilion where headhunters lie in wait for you to pause and make eye contact, and they leap on you and make you hear about the benefits of beautician training, the opportunities in the field of broadcasting.

The way to dry out your pants is to get on a motorized contraption that whirls you through the air. Your child suggests you ride the giant Slingshot that is across the street. A long line of dead-end kids wait to be strapped into a cage and flung straight up in the air. The mob of onlookers waiting for the big whoosh looks like the crowds that once gathered to watch public executions.

You pass up the Slingshot for the double Ferris wheel. An excellent clothes dryer, lifting you up above the honky-tonk, a nice breeze in your pants, in a series of parabolas, and at the apex you look out across the gaudy uproar and the blinking lights, and then you zoom down for a close-up of a passing gang of farm boys in green letter jackets and then back up in the air. You tell your child that this Ferris wheel is the ride that, going back to childhood, you always saved for last, and so riding it fills you with nostalgia. She pats your hand. "You'll be all right, Dad," she says. After ten minutes you come down nice and dry, and also the food has settled in your stomach, and you're ready for seconds.

Of the ten Joys, the one that we Midwesterners are loath to cop to is number three, the mingling and jostling, a pleasure that Google and Facebook can't provide. American life tends more and more to put you in front of a computer screen in a cubicle, then into a car and head you toward home in the suburbs, where you drive directly into the garage and step into your kitchen without brushing elbows with anybody. People seem to want this, as opposed to urban tumult and squalor. But we have needs we can't admit, and one is to be in a scrum of thinly clad corpulence milling in brilliant sun in front of the deep-fried-ice-cream stand and feel the brush of wings, hip bumps, hands touching your arm ("Oh, excuse me!"), the heat of humanity with its many smells (citrus deodorant, sweat and musk, bouquet of beer, hair oil, stale cigar, methane), the solid, big-rump bodies of Brueghel peasants all around you like dogs in a pack, and you—yes, elegant you of the refined taste and the commitment to the arts—are one of these dogs. All your life you dreamed of attaining swanhood or equinity, but your fellow dogs know better. They sniff you and turn away, satisfied.

Some state fairs are roomier, some gaudier, but there is a great sameness to them, just as there is a similarity among Catholic churches. No state fair can be called trendy, luxurious, dreamy—none of that. Nothing that is farm oriented or pigcentric is even remotely upscale.

Wealth and social status aren't so evident at the fair. The tattooed carnies who run the rides have a certain hauteur, and of course if you're on horseback, you're aristocracy, but otherwise not. There is no first-class line, no concierge section roped off in the barns. The wine selection is white, red, pink, and fizzy. Nobody flaunts his money.

The state fair, at heart, is an agricultural expo, and farming isn't about getting rich, and farmers discuss annual income less than they practice nude meditation on beaches. Farming is about work and about there being a Right Way and a Wrong Way to do it. You sit in the bleachers by the show ring and see this by the way the young women and men lead their immaculate cows clockwise around the grumpy, baggy-pants judge in the center. They walk at the cow's left shoulder, hand on the halter, and keep the animal's head up, always presenting a clear profile to the judge's gaze, and when he motions them to get in line, the exhibitors stand facing their cows and keep them squared away.

You and I may have no relatives left in farming, and our memory of the farm, if we have any, may be faint, but the livestock judging is meaningful to us—husbandry is what we do, even if we call it education or health care or management. Sport is a seductive metaphor (life as a game in which we gain victory through hard work, discipline, and visualizing success), but the older metaphor of farming (life as hard labor that is subject to weather and quirks of blind fate and may return no reward whatsoever and don't be surprised) is still in our blood, especially those of us raised on holy scripture. The young men and women leading cows around the show ring are relatives of Abraham and Job and the faithful father of the prodigal son. They subscribe to the Love Thy Neighbor doctrine. They know about late-summer hailstorms. You could learn something from these people.

Twilight falls on the fairgrounds, and a person just suddenly gets sick of it all. You've spent hours gratifying yourself on deep-fried cheese curds, deep-fried ice cream, testing one sausage against another, washing them down with authentic American sarsaparilla, sampling your child's onion rings, postponing the honey sundae for later, and now it is later, and the horticulture building and the honey-sundae booth are four blocks and a river of humanity away. You and the child stand at the entrance to the midway, barkers barking at you to try the ringtoss, shoot a basketball, squirt the water in the clown's mouth and see the ponies run, win the teddy bear, but you don't want to win a big blue plush teddy bear. You have no use for one whatsoever. There is enough inertia in your life as it is. And now you feel the great joy of revulsion at the fair and its shallow pleasures, its cheap tinsel, its greasy food. You are slightly ashamed of your own intake of animal fats. Bleaugh, you think. Arghhhh. OMG. You have gone twice to ATMs to finance this binge, and you regret that. No more of this! You take the child's hand. There

When you're slammed through the night sky at 75 miles an hour and 4 g's, "your stomach stays on the ground," says Minnesota fairgoer Tim Petersen. Reluctant at first, he and Deborah Smith finally succumbed to the Slingshot's 200-foot launch and free fall to Earth. Go again? "Definitely."

will be no honey sundae tonight, honey. We got all that out of our system. We are going home and sober up and get busy.

You hike toward where you recollect you parked your car this morning, and by a stroke of God's grace you actually find it, and your child does not have to watch a father roaming around pitifully, moaning to himself. You get in, and you drive back to the world that means something, the world of work. The Long Dark Time is coming, and you must gather your herds to shelter and lay in carrots and potatoes in the cellar.

The fair is gone the next day, the rides disassembled, the concessions boarded up, the streets swept clean. Dry leaves blow across the racing oval, brown squirrels den up in the ticket booths, the midway marquee sways in the wind. You drive past the fairgrounds a few days later on your way to work. It looks like the encampment of an invading army that got what booty it wanted and went home. And now you are yourself again, ambitious, disciplined, frugal, walking briskly, head held high, and nobody would ever associate you with that shameless person stuffing his face with bratwurst and kraut, mustard on his upper lip, and a half-eaten deep-fried Snickers in his other hand. That was not the real you. This is. This soldier of the simple declarative sentence. You have no need for cheap glitter and pig fat and pointless twirling. You have work to do. Onward.

Discussion Questions

- What specific rhetorical techniques does Keillor use to invite the reader to accompany him to the fair? What descriptions are most striking—either alluring or repelling? How, then, does form interact with content and contribute to meaning in this essay?

- What do the top ten attractions of state fairs say about the nature of these events per se? What does the list say about Keillor?

- If the state fairs Keillor visits are representative of the Upper Midwest, is the Upper Midwest representative of the United States?

- Could an urban dweller "get" what state fairs are about?

Writing Activities

- Why does Keillor bring his child to the state fair? What does he himself gain from doing so? How does their going together express something essential about state fairs and contribute to the custom?

- How do animals and humans interact and intermingle, actually and metaphorically, at the fair? What details bring out these connections in the essay? What broader cultural themes does Keillor address through them?

- What is Keillor's idea of work and of the day-to-day world? What alternatives might there be?

- In considering this question, you may wish to compare ideas of "job satisfaction" that come up elsewhere in this reader (see, for example, "21st-Century Cowboys," and "Silicon Valley").

- "Recreation": the word can be used in many senses, in many contexts. Providing some definitions and illustrating them with examples, consider more broadly what purposes recreation serves individuals and society.

Collaborative Activities

- What regions of the country are represented in your classroom? What special events are associated with these regions? How do they compare to state fairs, as Keillor describes them?

- Food is, of course, a central feature of fairs and celebrations. What kinds of food are characteristic of special occasions in your family and community? Would you consider these to be "American" foods? And, more broadly, how are food and cultural identity related?

ZipUSA: HOT COFFEE ROAD, MS 39428; A JAVA JUNKIE'S QUEST FOR TRUE BREW

Seeking the perfect cup in a Mississippi area called "Hot Coffee Road," a self-professed java junkie has some interesting encounters with locals. His experiences there may also put some perspective on the ubiquity of coffee shop chains elsewhere these days.

As you read "A Java Junkie's Quest for True Brew," you should consider the following questions:

- What expectations does the title of the article raise?
- Does the article fulfill those expectations?

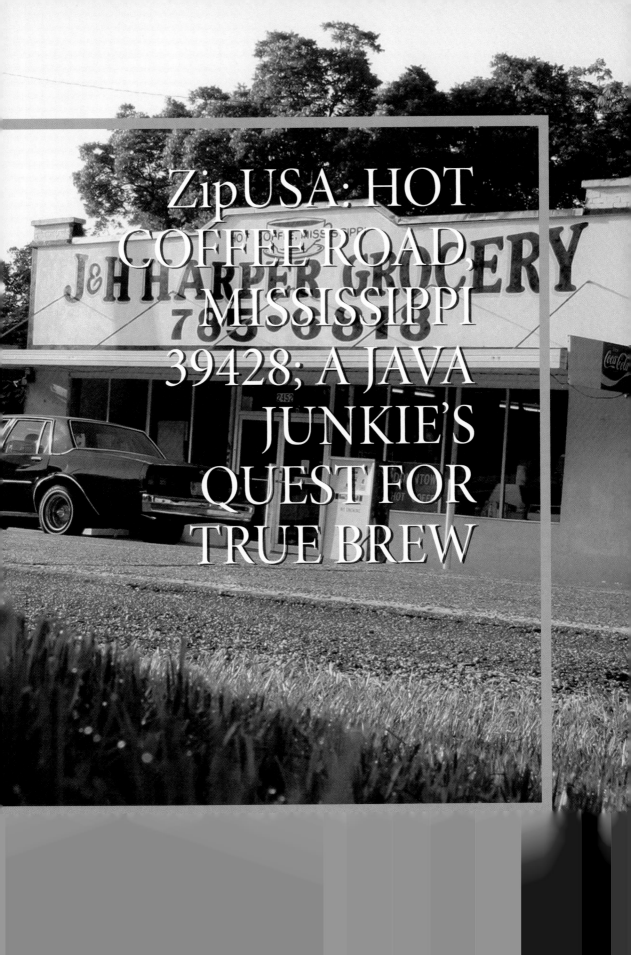

ZipUSA: HOT COFFEE ROAD, MISSISSIPPI 39428; A JAVA JUNKIE'S QUEST FOR TRUE BREW

Martha Diehl serves members of the Stevens family, who drove an hour and a half to indulge in roast beef and corn bread salad, cinnamon pears and coconut macaroon pie—all served family style at Martha's Kitchen, an old-fashioned dining hall on the Diehls' farm.

© 2005 Ira Block/National Geographic Image Collection

THE KEY TO TRUE BREW NIRVANA.

WILL HE FIND THE SECRET OR FIND THAT COFFEE HAS BEEN LONG GROUND INTO THE PAST?

Rio, a hundred-pound Czech shepherd, has locked his gaze on me as if I were a giant rabbit. He can barely contain himself. Quivering with anticipation, he emits high-pitched yelps, begging his master to utter the command that will launch him at me like a canine missile. Plainly put, he looks like a dog that's had one too many cups of coffee.

A police dog is not what I expected to find in Hot Coffee, Mississippi. As an avowed coffee junkie, I envisioned a quaint hamlet lined with tidy cafés serving all manner of frothy, caffeinated libations. The citizens of Hot Coffee would know their arabica beans from their robusta, grocery store off-brands would be outlawed, and the mayor might even be part Colombian. Perhaps there would be a coffee fountain in the town square. Forget Seattle, Vienna, and other self-proclaimed coffee capitals, I told myself. Hot Coffee, if only by the perfect simplicity of its name, must surely hold the key to true brew nirvana.

But when I got to Hot Coffee, about halfway between Jackson and Hattiesburg, reality was a cold shower. Hot Coffee isn't a quaint

Hot coffee, if only by the perfect simplicity of its name, must surely hold the key to true brew nirvana.

little town; it's not even a town. Instead it's a tiny community of farms, homes, and businesses scattered along two-lane Highway 532. The 12-mile stretch known locally as Hot Coffee Road runs from the town of Mount Olive to a crossroads that dates back to pioneer days. There, according to local lore, a resident opened an inn in 1870 and sold coffee to passersby. Apparently the drink was the only memorable thing about the place.

Which brings me back to Rio, whose owner lives in a house built on the site of the old inn. I'd knocked on the door, hoping to find coffee but found instead Pete Robinette. He and his wife moved from Hattiesburg to expand the kennel where Pete trains law enforcement dogs to sniff out drugs and apprehend suspects. It's this latter skill Pete offered to let Rio demonstrate—on me.

"You ready?" Pete calls. Rio leans forward. Although I'm wearing a heavily padded sleeve over my right arm—which Pete assures me is

Adapted from "ZipUSA: Hot Coffee Road, Mississippi, 39428; A Java Junkie's Quest for True Brew" by Peter Gwin: National Geographic Magazine, January 2005.

the only thing the dog will bite—my mind races. How in the name of Juan Valdez did a story about coffee become an episode of *Fear Factor*?

It's over before I know it. I vaguely recall offering the sleeve like a giant bone and Rio chomping it with the force of an alligator. I remove the sleeve and pet the panting dog, my arm throbbing. Pete is grinning. "You want to do it again?"

I politely decline and take my leave, hoping to find a coffee shop farther down the road. Instead I find a blueberry farm. I pull over, reasoning that where there are blueberries, there is pie, and where there is pie, there must be coffee.

Herman Neff, a rawboned 80-year-old with a long white beard, stands in the middle of his 60 acres of blueberry bushes, each laden with hundreds of plump, purple baubles. Over the low buzz of cicadas he explains the blueberry revolution sweeping this part of the state. His face lights up as he tells me how his neighbors thought he was crazy back in 1981 when he planted his first bushes, a special variety bred to withstand the Mississippi heat. "They don't think I'm crazy now," he says, tilting back his broad-brimmed straw hat. Many local farmers have joined him, and currently more than 800 acres in Covington County are covered in blueberry bushes.

Blueberries, Neff says, are a perfect food, veritable bomb-lets of antioxidants, which may help ward off cancer, and packed with other nutrients that some studies show will improve eyesight, reduce bad cholesterol, prevent urinary tract infections, and—ahem—keep one regular.

Neff never mentions pie, and before I can bring up the subject he's heading back to the chore at hand: harvesting his biggest crop in 23 years, more than 200 tons of blueberries. He and his two grandsons climb aboard a machine that resembles an automated car wash on wheels—a blueberry harvester. As

> Many local farmers have joined him, and currently more than 800 acres in Covington are covered in blueberry bushes.

they head down a row, the machine seems to swallow the eight-foot bushes, its fingerlike rods combing the branches, tickling ripe fruit into its belly.

I pop a handful of berries into my mouth, savoring their tangy juice in the midday heat. As the harvester chugs toward the horizon, Herman Neff is silhouetted against the blue sky. With his long beard and hat, he cuts the figure of a latter-day Ahab, cruising high above his sea of blueberries on a quest for a Moby Dick-size crop. While considering this thought, I recall that Ahab's first mate was named Starbuck.

My own quest culminates near the end of Hot Coffee Road, where I at last find a satisfying cup at Martha's Kitchen, an old-fashioned dining hall used for family reunions and other events. It's run by the Diehl family, who as Old Order German Baptists shun most modern conveniences, including electricity, telephones, and cars. "It's not that we believe these things are wrong," explains Martha, the daughter for whom the dining hall is named, "but they can create unnecessary temptations."

The Diehls don't seem to mind tempting me with food. Family matriarch Edith Diehl, dressed in a long skirt and a white bonnet despite the Mississippi heat, has laid in front of me a wedge of coconut macaroon pie that melts on my tongue with such decadent sweetness that it surely must violate a dozen biblical tenets.

Edith's husband, Bill, who has a long white beard similar to Herman Neff's, refills my coffee and explains his secret for brewing the perfect cup. "You never pour boiling water over the grounds," he tells me. "I learned that in the egg business. Lots of coffee drinkers in the egg business."

You don't want to get Bill started on the various businesses he has embarked on—that is, unless you have a big piece of pie in front of you. During the 25 years since they moved here from rural Maryland, the Diehls' enterprises have included a butchery, a bakery, and a produce stand. Today they grow fruits and vegetables, make baskets, quilts, and furniture, and, when the weather's not too hot, cook for large groups at Martha's Kitchen.

As Bill pours me another cup, I ask him what brought the family to Hot Coffee. He says friends told them land was cheap and the people friendly: "It sounded like a good place." I raise the steaming coffee to my lips and inhale the aroma. Indeed, it is.

Discussion Questions

- Does the author find a perfect cup of coffee on "Hot Coffee Road"? If so, what made it perfect for him? Would it be replicable anywhere else?

- Quests can take us in many different, unexpected directions, as this article attests. How does the organization of the article itself connect to the quest?

Writing Activities

- "Are you a coffee drinker?" Hosts often ask this question of their guests. Why is that? What do you make of the fact that it is a pretty routine query to make? What is your answer, and what does it say about you?

- While the question of "What's in a name?" has come up elsewhere in this reader, especially where personal identity is concerned (see, for example, "Changing America," as well as "Indian: Scenes from a Renaissance" and "Once Upon a Time in Laredo"), the question is also very much applicable to place. How does this article address and answer "What's in a name?" What further thoughts do you yourself have as well?

Collaborative Activities

- Compare Starbuck's and Dunkin' Donuts: What images and experiences do each of these chains project? How is their respective atmosphere similar to and/or different from neighborhood coffee shops and local cafes? How do you account for the popularity of the chains?

HOW WALT DISNEY CHANGED EVERYTHING

While millions of tourists throng through Disney World, the theme park is more than just a vacation destination. As T. D. Allman demonstrates, not only did Walt Disney's enterprise radically affect the physical, social, and economic landscape of central Florida, his "Magic Kingdom" also set a precedent for the exurbs that sprawl all over the country and the forces of franchising that influence so much of American culture today.

As you read "How Walt Disney Changed Everything," you should consider the following questions:

- Before reading the article, think about some ideas and/or experiences that the "World of Walt Disney" conjures up for you. As you read on, do you find that your perspective corresponds with the author's?

- After you've read the essay, do you want to go to Orlando? Do you feel as though you're already there?

Buyers of homes along Orlando's Old Patina Way get to choose from an array of earth-toned colors.

HOW WALT DISNEY CHANGED EVERY- THING

Photographs by David Burnett

For 13-year-olds Paige Phillips, left, and Abbey Key, of Oxford, Alabama, Disney World is a once-in-a-childhood pilgrimage, a dream come true. Seventy million people a year visit Orlando theme parks.

ORLANDO IS THE
NEW
AMERICAN
METROPOLIS.

> **O**rlando's explosion is visible in every shopping mall and traffic jam. **You can also see it from outer space.**

Everything happening to America today is happening here, and it's far removed from the cookie-cutter suburbanization of life a generation ago. The Orlando region has become Exhibit A for the ascendant power of our cities' exurbs: blobby coalescences of look-alike, overnight, amoeba-like concentrations of population far from city centers. These huge, sprawling communities are where more and more Americans choose to be, the place where job growth is fastest, home building is briskest, and malls and megachurches are multiplying as newcomers keep on coming. Who are all these people? They're you, they're me, and increasingly, they are nothing like the blue-eyed "Dick and Jane" of mythical suburban America.

Orlando's explosion is visible in every shopping mall and traffic jam. You can also see it from outer space. When Earth satellites were first launched, Florida photographed at night looked like two l's standing side by side: One long string of lights ran down the Atlantic side of the peninsula; another ran along the Gulf of Mexico side. In between was darkness. Today the two parallel l's have become a lopsided *H*. Central Florida glows as though a phosphorescent creature from outer space has landed there and started reproducing. It gobbles up existing communities even as it transforms scrub and swamp into a characterless conurbation of congested freeways and parking lots. All of this is "Orlando," the brand name for this region of two million residents.

When people tell the story of Orlando's stunning transformation from swamp and sinkhole to 21st-century metropolis, they begin, inevitably, with the man and the mouse. The mouse is Mickey, the man Walt Disney. If it weren't for Disney, the local saying goes, the Orlando region would be called Ocala, a rival town up the road. Disney first flew over central Florida in an airplane chartered under an alias to keep his mission

Adapted from "How Walt Disney Changed Everything"
by T.D. Allman: National Geographic Magazine,
March 2007.

In Red Lobster's test kitchen—birthplace of popcorn shrimp—dishes are tasted again and again en route from the Orlando corporate headquarters to menus at 682 locations nationwide. "We ask, 'Does it move our brand forward?'" says corporate chef Michael LaDuke, third from left.

secret. It was the fateful day of November 22, 1963. The Kennedy assassination would mark America forever. So would the decision Walt Disney made that day to turn an inland Florida agricultural center into an epicenter of world tourism.

Orlando was the county seat of Orange County, but it wasn't citrus groves that prompted Disney's secret aerial reconnaissance. During his flyover, he focused on a wasteland southwest of Orlando where alligators outnumbered people. Porous limestone underlay the vegetal muck. What passed for dry land was speckled with shallow, brown-watered catchments, some the size of station wagons, others the size of suburbs. "That's it," Disney proclaimed,

pointing down to the future site of what he dreamed of creating in this Florida wilderness: Epcot, America's Experimental Prototype Community of Tomorrow.

Over the next two years, with the collusion of Orlando's top leaders, Disney secretly acquired more than 25,000 acres. People were glad to sell dirt cheap. This sludgy terrain was useless for agriculture. It was far from Florida's beaches. It was hot and muggy most of the year, yet it got so cold during central Florida's brief winters that deep freezes periodically killed the citrus crop.

Who would want to vacation in such a place? Disney was certain most Americans would, once he worked his marketing magic on them. By the 1960s, all over America, suburbs were replacing old neighborhoods. Malls were driving Main Street out of business. There was hardly a new ranch home or split-level that didn't have a TV antenna on the roof. Disney realized that in the coming decades shows like *The Mickey Mouse Club,* not climate and geology, would determine what the majority of Americans would consider a safe and enjoyable place to take a family vacation. That day, flying over central Florida, Disney decided that he, not reality, would define what constituted the Magic Kingdom in the minds and spending habits of millions of Americans in the years to come.

The interstate highway system, started by the Eisenhower Administration as part of the Cold War defense effort against communism, was already crisscrossing America. Disney chose Orlando because it was at the confluence of two of the most important of these new thoroughfares, what today are Interstate 4 and Florida's Turnpike. There was also a deeply personal reason he located Disney World there—the same one that still lures people to Orlando today. In Florida's boggy, buggy, empty midsection, Walt Disney perceived a second chance.

His original theme park—Disneyland, in southern California—covered fewer than 300 acres. It soon was ringed with the suburban blight that its success inevitably attracted—motels, strip malls, copycat amusement parks. Disney never forgave himself for not making Disneyland big enough, but in Florida he hoped to rectify that mistake. He set out to create an Adventureland where nothing was left to chance. Arriving visitors would not be permitted to choose their own parking spaces; smiling Disney characters would do that for them. In this new, bigger, better Magic Kingdom, water could not be the tannic brown common in central Florida. So Bay Lake was drained, the sludge removed, and clear water pumped into the resulting lagoon. Even dry land would be turned into another Disney illusion: As you traverse the theme park, you are actually walking on the roof of

an immense, underground control building from which the operation is run, staffed, and supplied.

Disney's new empire in central Florida would be marketed as Disney World. Its official name was, and remains, the Reedy Creek Improvement District. Thanks to a sweetheart deal with the state legislature, the lands Disney purchased were detached from the rest of Florida to form a Magic Kingdom, above and outside the law. Even now, Disney World's rides are exempt from state safety inspections. Democratic process is excluded, too. Power remains in the hands of a board of supervisors composed of Disney allies. However much you pay for a time-share condo in Disney World, you cannot buy property outright, and therefore establish official residence, and therefore vote for the board. Celebration, Disney's residential community themed to evoke pre-1940s small-town America, has a city hall but no actual municipal government.

In this place of exurban, postmodern pioneers, the range of choices is vast even when the choices themselves are illusory. Here life is truly a style: You don't want to live in a mass-produced, instant "community"? No problem. Orlando's developers, like the producers of instant coffee, offer you a variety of flavors, including one called Tradition. Structurally it may seem identical to all the others. Only instead of vaguely Mediterranean ornamental details, the condos at Tradition have old colonial finishes. In Orlando's lively downtown, it's possible to live in a loft just as you would in Chicago or New York. But these lofts are brand-new buildings constructed for those who want the postindustrial lifestyle in a place that never was industrial.

Orlando's bright lights are not the garish displays of Las Vegas or the proud power logos of New York. Instead, Orlando glimmers with the familiar signage of franchise America: Denny's, Burger King, Quality Inn, Hampton Inn, Hertz. Orlando also leads in the culinary transformation of the exotic into the familiar. From its Orlando headquarters, the Darden Corporation, the city's first *Fortune* 500 company, mass-markets theme foods. It standardizes the output of Red Lobsters and Olive Gardens everywhere.

All over Orlando you see forces at work that are changing America from Fairbanks to Little Rock. This, truly, is a 21st-century paradigm: It is growth built on consumption, not production; a society founded not on natural resources, but upon the dissipation of capital accumulated elsewhere; a place of infinite possibilities, somehow held together, to the extent it is held together at all, by a shared recognition of highway signs, brand names, TV shows, and personalities, rather than any shared history. Nowhere else is the juxtaposition of what America actually is and the conventional idea of what America should be more vivid and revealing.

Welcome to the theme-park nation.

Very few people, as they talk about the immense changes reshaping Orlando and their lives, mention another American genius who left his mark here even before Disney arrived. Jack Kerouac—guru, bad boy, the literary superstar who wrote the Beat Generation's manifesto, *On The Road*—came to Orlando, by bus, in December 1956. The following year, in an 11-day creative frenzy, he wrote *The Dharma Bums* in an apartment with a tangerine tree out back, shoveling the words through his typewriter in the heart of hot, flat Florida.

Kerouac's tumultuous vision was a howling rant against the plastic shackles he perceived imprisoning the human spirit in mid-century America. Looking out his window at the neighbors, he scorned "the middle-class non-identity which finds its perfect expression ... in rows of well-to-do houses with lawns and television sets in each living room with

Around the world, Orlando is synonymous with the theme-park culture that has overtaken America.

everybody looking at the same thing and thinking the same thing at the same time." Whereas Disney was looking for control, Kerouac personified the American urge to defy control. Disney acted out the old American idea that if you can just grab hold of enough American wilderness, you can create a world free of the problems that besiege people in places like the frost belt. Kerouac evoked a rootless America where, no matter how far people wander, they never reach their destination.

Never were two men so totally American and so totally different, yet both of them wound up in Orlando. This prophetic convergence raises the question: When it came to America's future, who was the better prophet of what, since then, we and our country have become? As a people, and as a nation, are we more like Disney's smiling "characters"? Or do we more resemble half-lost wanderers, like Kerouac and his crew?

The answer seems clear: Around the world, Orlando is synonymous with the theme-park culture that has overtaken America. Nowhere else does the triumph of the Disney ethos seem so total, yet something paradoxical emerges when you get to know the place. Fifty years on, Kerouac's restless spirit is still on the loose in Orlando's discount shopping malls. It prowls the RV parks and hangs out at the fast-food franchises. Wherever people neglect to mow the grass, or curse the car payments, you're in Kerouac's Orlando because they, like him, were once from someplace else. And, for a while at least, Orlando seemed to them, as it did to the Beat apostle, like a place where the utility bills never get past due and the past can never haunt you.

"Why not come to Orlando and dig the crazy Florida scene of spotlessly clean highways and fantastic supermarkets?" Kerouac wrote Lawrence Ferlinghetti, the Beat poet, in 1961. But in Orlando, as everywhere else he

Streetlamps mark the future homes of Savannah Landings, a development on Orlando's east edge where town houses named Scarlett and Ashley will go for $236,000 and up. Best perk in a far-flung city with no trains and few buses: easy access to Route 417.

roamed, Kerouac never did find escape. Florida became for him, after he stopped writing, a place to drink, and ultimately a place to die. The little house at 1418 Clouser Avenue where Kerouac wrote his novel now serves as a kind of literary time-share, where writers spend three months at a stint, hoping to channel Kerouac's manic genius.

Things did not turn out as Walt Disney intended either. People thronged to the Magic Kingdom to see with their own eyes what they'd seen on TV, but Epcot, Disney's cherished project of creating a futuristic community where people lived and worked in high-tech harmony, never became a reality. People weren't interested in Disney's edgeless version of tomorrow. Epcot was such a failure that Disney officials faced the embarrassing prospect of shutting it down. Instead, they turned it into another tourist attraction. Today

Epcot offers a nostalgic pastiche of a 1940s seashore vacation 60 miles from the nearest sea, along with food options themed to places like Gay Paree, a space ride, and "Key West" time-share options.

By trying to create a Magic Kingdom immune from squalor and complexity, Disney touched off an orgy of uncontrolled growth that still shows no signs of abating. Extinct theme parks litter the Orlando landscape the way dead factories mark the rust belt. Defunct attractions like Splendid China, which featured a miniature Great Wall, went bankrupt because they were too realistic. They failed to provide what all successful theme parks must: fantasies conforming exactly to what the paying public expects to get.

Today Orlando is a cauldron of all the communal characteristics Disney sought to control. In its Parramore district, you can stock up on crack, meth, and angel dust. According to the Morgan Quitno research firm, in 2006 it joined such cities as Detroit and St. Louis to become one of the 25 most dangerous cities in America. The result is armed guards at the gates of "communities" where entry is solely by invitation. The Orlando area also has one of the highest pedestrian death rates among the largest metro regions in the country. Four decades after Disney's fateful flyover, Orlando is a place of enormous vitality, diversity, ugliness, discord, inventiveness, possibility, and disappointed hopes, where no clown in a character costume can tell people how to live, let alone where to park.

These days Orlando is as multicultural as New York, and as much in the throes of globalization as any import-export center. Its growth has brought people speaking more than 70 languages to central Florida. Kissimmee, south of Orlando and just east of Disney World, has gone from being a cowboy town to mostly Hispanic in less than ten years. The tentacles of diversity have penetrated Disney World too. Few tourists realize it, but when their kids hug Goofy and Minnie they might be embracing low-wage workers from places like Sri Lanka and the Dominican Republic.

Some complain the newcomers from developing countries aren't "real Americans." Others complain the newcomers from up north aren't "real Floridians." "We have drive-by citizens," says Linda Chapin, a former Orange County commissioner. People move to Florida, but they don't bring their loyalties with them. In such a situation of psychological rootlessness and moral detachment, the question isn't whether the problems arising from unchecked growth can be solved. It's whether there is any chance of them being addressed at all.

"We've allowed Florida to be turned into a strip mall," says Chapin. "This is our great

We've allowed Florida to be turned into a strip mall. This is our great tragedy.

tragedy." While she was head of the county commission, she played a major role in unleashing Orlando's nonstop building boom. She masterminded Orlando's new convention center, along with other projects intended to assure an influx of people into the area. "My name is in gold letters over at the convention center," she says. "It makes my mother proud." These days, as head of urban planning at the University of Central Florida, she thinks up ways to slow down Orlando's growth, and humanize it.

Chapin talks about the reasons why, back in the beginning, change and growth seemed like such unalloyed blessings. "We thought we could manage growth," she says. In her lifetime, a sky's-the-limit scenario has turned Orlando into a city of suburban, and human, dilemmas. Still, this is can-do America. As Chapin, suddenly reverting to optimism, puts it: "Just because we've ruined 90 percent of everything doesn't mean we can't do wonderful things with the remaining ten percent!"

You can see Orlando's sprawl from outer space. Go to Cypress Creek High and Meadow Woods Middle School, and you see the human complexity in the eyes of its students. The sky was streaked dawn pink as I headed out to the moving edge of Orlando. Fifteen miles southwest of downtown, I reached the latest spot where central Florida's population explosion has turned wilderness into tract housing overnight. If the moon were ever settled, this is how it would be done. Whole neighborhoods, consisting of hundreds of houses, arrived here instantly. So have the people who live in them.

Demographically, these two schools match the Orlando area. Here both whites and blacks are in the minority; "other" is the dominant ethnicity. I picked them because they are typical schools, but when I visited I found

Debate students at Orlando's Cypress Creek High speak six languages besides English—Hindi, Gujarati, Urdu, Mandarin, Japanese, and Creole. As immigrants pass up gateway cities like Miami for better schools and affordable homes, suburbs are no longer homogenous enclaves.

something extraordinary—two places where more than 8,000 students and teachers were finding new ways to learn, and new ways to live together.

At Cypress Creek and Meadow Woods, great events are not just things these kids and their teachers see on TV. They impinge on people's lives. At Cypress Creek, the assistant principal, Vanessa Colon Schaefer, was still putting her life back together after more than a year in Iraq. When her National Guard unit was sent there, she left a gap in the life of her daughter, and of this school. Kids from nearly 200 countries study at the two schools. "Normally they shout out their countries when I ask them," says Chuck Rivers, the principal at Meadow Woods. "But

one time a little boy just whispered. When I asked him again, he kept whispering, so I bent down to hear him. He whispered 'Iraq' in my ear." Rivers adds, with no false sentimentality, "They're all my kids."

I talk to students from Colombia, Brazil, Haiti, Jamaica, Korea, China, the Philippines, Iran, Russia, Slovakia, and India—and I've just begun to plumb the mutations. "My mother is from Germany," one little girl says, "and my father is from Madagascar." Diversity is not an objective, or a program, or a lifestyle here. It is life.

At Cypress Creek I talk with the school's National Merit Scholars. I visit classes where kids are autistic or deaf or otherwise different. I sense how important it is for children to find themselves integrated, every day, with kids who are different from them mentally, physically, racially, culturally. The principal of Cypress Creek is a woman; the principal of Meadow Woods is black. He remembers the days of racial segregation. Now he is in charge of a learning experience where racial barriers aren't the only things that have become meaningless. No dumbing down is going on here. At the middle school, kids are studying things I never learned in all my years of schooling: how to conduct a symphony, how blood circulates, how to fix a faucet, how to solve disputes openly and nonviolently. As we leave, the principal says something that sticks in my mind: "We do this every day."

One morning i have what people in Orlando call the I-4 experience. I zoom off in my car for a midday appointment. It turns into an afternoon appointment by the time I get there. For most of an hour, every car sits motionless. For the first time I truly understand what people mean when they call I-4 "Orlando's parking lot." Nothing is more obvious than the need for a light-rail system connecting Disney, downtown, the airport, and points in between. But in Orlando people love their cars as much as they hate paying taxes. Orlando's roads, so recently slashed through the wilderness, are already deteriorating.

Being stuck in traffic gives you time to think; I wind up thinking about how different Orlando's image of itself is from reality. The irony of Orlando is that people go there in search of Disneyesque tranquillity—and by doing so, they've unleashed upon the place all the rootless, restless contradictions of America. Here is big city traffic, big city crime, yet people in Orlando cherish the idea that they have escaped the trials people face in other cities. On this morning, it is cold, so cold I turn the car heater to high—though at most times of year it is stultifyingly hot. Ahead of me is an overpass, and just to complete the refutation of Orlando's all-American self-image, a big semi lunges across the overpass. "Lucky Noodles," giant red characters proclaim, both in English and Chinese; it is carrying supplies for Orlando's Asian supermarkets.

For some reason the truck with the graceful Chinese writing on it reminds me of the lyrics of that old Disney theme song:

When you wish upon a star
Makes no difference who you are
Anything your heart desires
Will come to you.

"If your heart is in your dream," the song goes on to allege, "No request is too extreme."

Discussion Questions

- What was Disney's vision for Orlando? How was it realized? How have the ensuing growth and development of Orlando conformed to his plans? How have they diverged?

- What are some of the striking words and images associated with nature in this article and how do they contribute to broader thematic conflicts such as control versus contingency or fantasy versus reality?

- Why was the residential scheme of America's Experimental Prototype Community of Tomorrow (Epcot) a failure? At the same time, even though people did not choose to live there, can the scheme be said to have been in some ways successful?

- In discussing forces of homogenization versus those of diversification, both in Orlando and in the broader American landscape, what kinds of evidence does Allman bring to bear to illustrate these tendencies? Does the article suggest that one or the other is stronger? How and why?

Writing Activities

- Pointing to the growing population of exurban dwellers, Allman asks, "Who are all these people?" and answers, "They're you. They're me." How would you yourself reply to Allman's assertion?

- After juxtaposing Jack Kerouac and Walt Disney, Allman wonders, "When it came to America's future, who was the better prophet of what, since then, we and our country have become? As a people, and as a nation, are we more like Disney's smiling 'characters'? Or do we more resemble half-lost wanderers, like Kerouac and his crew?" What would you say?

- Compare the place where you grew up—whether in the country or in the city, in a village or town, in suburbia or exurbia, in the United States or elsewhere--with that of Orlando. Are there any striking similarities and/or differences? What might some of the implications be?

- What do you make of Allman's observation that Disney World is "an adventureland where nothing [is] left up to chance"? As you analyze the meaning and implications of this phrase, consider whether and to what extent other features of American culture exemplify this quality.

Collaborative Activities

- "Life, liberty, and the pursuit of happiness": Does Disney World exemplify these American principles, or undermine them?

- Using the Internet, identify three or four major attractions at Disney World and divide them among study groups. After each group learns as much as possible about its topic--including perhaps taking a virtual tour--each should consider what is, and is not, attractive about the chosen feature. Then, groups can compare notes, as well as further thoughts about the nature of the appeal of Disney World.

21ST-CENTURY COWBOYS: WHY THE SPIRIT ENDURES

The danger and the drudgery of this job are no less than they were a century ago. Having no electricity or running water is the least of it. And the pay is negligible too. So why would anyone want to be a cowboy in the 21st century? This article examines what can, for some, be the draw of this way of life.

As you read "21st-Century Cowboys: Why the Spirit Endures," you should consider the following questions:

- What images and ideas of cowboys do you have? Where do these come from?
- Just looking at the photographs that accompany this article, what do they suggest about cowboys? As you read, consider the relationship between image and text.

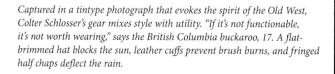

Captured in a tintype photograph that evokes the spirit of the Old West, Colter Schlosser's gear mixes style with utility. "If it's not functionable, it's not worth wearing," says the British Columbia buckaroo, 17. A flat-brimmed hat blocks the sun, leather cuffs prevent brush burns, and fringed half chaps deflect the rain.

21ST-CENTURY COWBOYS: WHY THE SPIRIT ENDURES

Photographs by Robb Kendrick

Beau and Rowdy Hall play basketball, swim, and snowboard, but cowboying on Colorado's North Pueblo Ranch alongside their father is the most fun of all. "They're more help than some of the grown-ups he's hired," says their mother.

FEW COWBOYS EVER OWNED MUCH.
THE PRIMARY REWARD OF BEING A COWBOY
WAS THE PLEASURE OF LIVING A COWBOY'S LIFE.

American cowboys have not vanished in the mists of legend.

There are two things that Wes Miner hopes not to see when he wakes early each morning and saddles up to survey the cattle left in his care. He does not wish to see a big black bird. Miner has nothing against crows or buzzards per se. But to view them wheeling solemnly across the sky, or scattering from the brush at his approach, is to feel his stomach tighten as he reckons with the knowledge that one or more of the animals entrusted to him have been killed.

Some of them are freak deaths. Four years ago, Miner worked on a ranch in Idaho where a spectacular electrical storm had erupted and toppled a dozen head of cattle huddled under a tree. Their bleached bones remained arrayed on the pasture for years as a testament to ill fortune. On the ranch he now tends in southwestern Montana, wolves devour a calf in the dark of night and leave no trace of the carnage. A cow gets stuck in a bog, breaks her leg, and Miner is forced to shoot her on the spot. A yearling munches on the blossoms of poisonous larkspur and drops dead within four hours. Nature gives and snatches away on a whim, but Wes Miner can handle that.

"What gets to me," says the 28-year-old somber-eyed cowboy, "is if we lose a bunch of sick ones. Because that's something I should control better."

Men in Wes Miner's trade love the riding, the roping, and the stark romanticism of a cow camp. But there is a bottom line, and it comes at the end of October, when the 4,100 head he is paid to tend are herded into corrals, and the cattle owners roll up in their dusty pickups to count and inspect their property.

In high country like the Snowline Ranch where Miner works, temperatures can see saw from 80 to 8 in a single day, and so pneumonia is a constant threat. It occupies Miner's attention as he rides through the cattle. If some of them get caught in a downpour during cold weather, he's fatally behind the curve. He must seize upon the earliest symptom: that lone calf amid the lurching sea of fur and fat with a single drooping ear, at which point Miner's horse separates the

Adapted from "21st-Century Cowboys: Why the Spirit Endures" by Robert Draper: National Geographic Magazine, December 2007.

calf from the others and the cowboy swings his long rope. Catch the calf with the first loop, reach for the meds in the saddlebag, inject the Nuflor. Done right, the calf barely notices, returns to the herd, and by the end of October is 600 pounds and received by his owner with an approving half smile—which to Wes Miner is a tiny miracle, at least compared with the sickly vision of the big black birds dining off his failures.

It's a proud feeling, knowing he has staved off tragedy and been rewarded with the gratitude of owners who wave goodbye as they cart off their fattened commodities. The satisfaction lasts an evening. The next morning comes, and with it Wes Miner faces the second spectacle that he would rather not see. It's the sight of a pasture with no cattle grazing on it. And this, too, feels like a sort of death. "We go so hard those last two or three weeks—every day, go, go, GO … and then you look on the hills, and there's nothing but those saddle horses. It's an empty feeling."

American cowboys have not vanished in the mists of legend. Against the howling locomotion of modern and postmodern and transmodern eras, they reside right where they have been for three centuries and counting: in the cattle country of the West and Southwest, and at the core of a nation's identity. This, despite the vagueness of the vocation itself. Are there ten thousand working cowboys today? Fifty thousand? Even were everyone to agree on the definition of "working cowboy"—and good luck with that—tracking the species has eluded every organization from the Working Ranch Cowboys Association to the United States Census Bureau.

Whatever the actual number, the job itself has gotten no easier in recent times. As cattle

With the hand-to-mouth lifestyle and the desire for independence comes an unexpected though endearing vanity: Cowboys care about how they look.

ranching has increasingly become big business, the cowboy's essential place is more subject to an accountant's dispassionate scrutiny. For that matter, the 71-billion-dollar U.S. cattle industry itself is beset by challenges from changing weather patterns, the vagaries of the international market, urban sprawl, and health threats from abroad. Inevitably, some cattle operations have learned to diversify by leasing out their acreage to hunters or offering dude-ranch tourism. Computerization—for ear-tagging and brand recording, among other uses—has increasingly become a welcome if strange bedfellow on cattle ranches.

But if high technology is the unstoppable force, here is the immovable object: Cattle subsist largely on grass. Cows need to be led to where the grass is ample. To achieve that requires no more and no less than an individual on horseback, accompanied by a rope and maybe a decent stock dog or two—all set on a landscape detached from urban clamor, not to mention cell phone service.

Proof of the cowboy's resilience is that he has survived Hollywood's ceaseless hyping of him as the quintessence of terse, masculine individuality. In the romanticizing, a few details are overlooked: Subzero February mornings. Triple-digit August afternoons. Cracked ribs from being bucked off a spooked horse. Thumbs severed by a roped steer. Forearms gooey from pushing a cow's prolapsed uterus back up into its vagina. And day after day, week after week spent watching a thousand furry creatures chew up a pasture while your own stomach growls. All of this for a wage that works out to about four dollars an hour. What this arrangement guarantees is self-selection. Only those who seek out such misery will endure it.

"Oh, yeah, it was fun," says 18-year-old Tyrel Tucker as he reflects on the winter he spent

Men who spend all day on horseback are particular about saddles. "Over the years, you figure out what works best for you," says Pat Crisswell (right) who uses a Texas-style swell-fork saddle on a Wyoming ranch. Chad Milius favors a buckaroo-style slick-fork rig.

with his 20-year-old brother, Blaine, tending 2,300 cattle in a camp north of Flagstaff. The brothers slept in a cinder-block shack with cracks in the walls and no electricity. Every day from December until April, they rode on nearly 100,000 acres of land with only the cattle, the horses, and each other for company. Blaine's cooking regimen did not vary: pancakes and sausage for breakfast, a can of sardines for lunch, potatoes and a hamburger on a biscuit or tortilla for dinner. The wind was relentless, and by nightfall the temperatures plummeted to 15 below zero.

None of which mattered. "We got to rope at least one calf every day," says Tyrel. "You get to be by yourself. Do your own thing, don't get bothered by the boss. I'd go back again."

The Tucker brothers are lanky and taciturn and uninterested in any other life save the one they have led since infancy, when they rode horseback before they were able to walk and received their first horses by the age of two. Not for sport, however: Their mother, Michelle, tended the family ranch near Powell, Wyoming, and needed her boys' help. When Tyrel was 17, he volunteered to drop out in the middle of his sophomore year of high school to get his GED and work full-time on the ranch. "It was great with me," Tyrel recalls. What was there to miss? All of his classmates spent their free time playing Nintendo.

Blaine wears a Fu Manchu mustache, as do his father and his uncle. Tyrel is still working on his. With the hand-to-mouth lifestyle and the desire for independence comes an unexpected though endearing vanity: Cowboys care about how they look. A man who drifts from

Native American cowgirls Harli and Ashley Cota (left and center) and Jessica Kelly rope and ride on the Duck Valley Indian Reservation in Nevada. Ashley, now 19, is studying ranch management to help her family market their hormone-free beef.

ranch to ranch, camp to camp, may not ever own a bed, much less a house. What he wears and what he straddles are pretty much all he's got. "You can do this job in tennis shoes and a ball cap, I guess," acknowledges Pat Crisswell, a compact Oklahoman who now tends a camp on the 150,000-acre Wagonhound Land and Livestock Company ranch in Wyoming. "But the more old-timey, the better."

The original vaqueros—derived from *vaca*, Spanish for "cow"—were horsemen from present-day Mexico who drove cattle into Texas and up into California. Replete with engraved silver and embellished leather gear, the vaqueros cut gallant figures on the surly canvas of the Old West. But form was seldom without function. Their flat-brimmed

hats and bandannas warded off the sun and the dust. And for durability, no cotton rope could compete against a hand-braided rawhide riata.

The vaquero style lives on in varying degrees in different regions. Mexico, with its sagging economy, is no longer chief custodian. Instead, California and Nevada buckaroos (itself a corruption of vaquero) are most apt to follow the tradition to the letter: half chaps, flashy silver bits, wide, flat-bottomed stirrups, slick-fork saddles, and the compulsory long ropes and flat hats. To the buckaroos, finesse is key. Rather than constantly jabbing, the buckaroo prefers to cue his horse with his spurs. The uncorrupted art of cattle roping—and God strike a cowboy dead for doctoring a sick cow from a four-wheeler instead of with a horse and lasso—involves first catching the cow, then dallying, or wrapping one's rope around the saddle horn rather than tying it on. This takes more time, but the buckaroo does it anyway, without apology.

"I like the slower pace—throw a big, purty loop, not a hurry-up deal where you're cussing at people," says Wes Miner, the Montana native who was reared in the rodeo trade and now cleaves to the buckaroo ways—as do others less devoted. He notes ruefully: " I wore the flat hat for years. Then one day in Bozeman I saw two guys wearing ones like mine. Turned out they worked for a gardening store."

Buckaroos are afforded their style by the wide-open terrain on which they labor. More rough-hewn landscapes breed a correspondingly unfussy approach to a cowboy's work and dress. Brush country tears up jeans, necessitating the full-length but unadorned shotgun-style chaps worn by cowboys (sometimes called cowpunchers) in the Great Plains states and Texas. Brushy, tree-cluttered environs require shorter ropes and swell-fork saddles to tie on to. (Dallying is, well, dallying.) In windy areas, a stiff gale can knock a flat hat off a cowboy's head, so he may prefer the steadier taco hat. Buckaroo purists may disparage the spartan, gritty style of cowpunchers as "hard and fast" and "rammin'-jammin'." (The term cowpuncher probably derives from the brisk manner in which 19th-century ranch hands loaded cattle onto trains.) But looks deceive. The care in a cowpuncher's work is as evident as in the more stylized rendition of the buckaroo's.

Tyrel Tucker did not know much about these loose distinctions among cowboy traditions until his brother, Blaine, returned from summer on a ranch near Pryor, Montana. The buckaroos there wore silver-studded half chaps, reined their steeds with twisted

Not every cowboy is born into the life. Some are loved into it.

horsehair mecates, and swung long rawhide ropes. So, now, do the Tucker brothers. Tyrel spends his free time working with silver, designing belt buckles and bits and spurs. The way other young men obsess over sports teams or computer games, Tyrel and Blaine Tucker devour every granule of the cowboy culture.

Not every cowboy is born into the life. "Some are loved into it," says Pat Crisswell, a racehorse jockey's son. "I had a government security job. The money was great, but I didn't like the city, and I spent more time in bars than I should've. So I went to the Pitchfork Ranch in Guthrie, Texas. Went from $20 an hour to $750 a month. Guys I left behind thought I was crazy. I told 'em, 'There's a little somethin' called job satisfaction.'"

The cowboy culture is more egalitarian than most. You can find boilerplate Westerners riding cattle—but also African Americans, Mexicans, Canadians, and even Mennonites, not to mention emigrants from Germany, Brazil, Australia, and even India. Most who heed the call are young single males stirred by the outdoorsman's yearning for manly adventure. But of course there are cowgirls, too, like Jodi Miner, a clear-eyed woman with a formidable handshake who grew up on a ranch near Dell, Montana, doctoring calves, repairing water tanks, and mending fences. In between college semesters at Bozeman, she took jobs calving and branding heifers and slept in bunkhouses surrounded by snoring men. Today, she and her husband, Wes, run the Snowline Ranch together on behalf of an absentee board of directors. They get free housing for themselves and their two young daughters. In return, the board expects Wes and Jodi Miner to devote themselves to ranch management, dealing with the Bureau of Land Management and the Forest Service. Cowboys have long been gypsy-like in their meanders—ever searching, through word of mouth (cowboys don't Google), for that optimal blend of agreeable terrain, independence, and the opportunity to stay in the saddle. "In Montana, there aren't many straight-up cowboy jobs anymore," sighs Wes Miner. "For the most part, you're gonna have to get off your horse a bit."

So the Miners, and most of their ilk, get off their horses. Adapt they must, when they must. Cowboys have seen the alternative to their life, from a safe distance: men who live for the weekend, for their golf game. There is no Monday or Friday out on the ranch. There is no "hobby." Instead, there is just being on a horse among three hundred elk and watching the sun rise. Cowboys don't rhapsodize about such pleasures. Leave that to the poets or the keen brilliance of artist Charlie Russell. The cowboys hold their passion in reserve—waiting till the snows melt and the cattle trailers pull up to the gates, followed by the year's first swell of hoofbeats. Then the vaqueros fall out of time, and they're riding and hollering, boys for one more season.

Discussion Questions

- According to Draper, cowboys continue to be "at the core of a nation's identity." What are the characteristics of cowboys? What national traits do they represent? How do these correspond with other ideas of American identity in this reader? And in your own view?

- One appeal of the life of the cowboy is, as one cowboy himself says, "You get to be by yourself. Do your own thing, don't get bothered by the boss." At the same time, cowboys are certainly tied to a bottom line, as Draper demonstrates. Is the freedom of cowboys illusory, then?

- What other contradictions surface in this article? Do they pertain only to cowboys, or do they resonate in the broader culture as well?

- "The cowboy culture is more egalitarian than most," writes Draper. In what ways does he support this position? Do you also find evidence that runs counter to it?

Writing Activities

- If Hollywood "hyped" cowboys as "the quintessence of terse, masculine individuality," how, and to what extent, does life imitate art amongst 21st-century cowboys, as portrayed by Draper?

- Taking up the question of gender from another point of view, what are the some of the characteristics of cowgirls? Do the qualities required by the job transcend gender, or not?

- Consider another image of the cowboy—that of the outlaw—and explore what being an "outlaw" represents in the United States.

- "Job satisfaction": What does the cowboy who refers to this mean? What would make a job satisfying to you? You may wish to compare other ideas of work found in this reader (including "Take in the State Fair with Garrison Kiellor" and "Silicon Valley").

Collaborative Activities

- Research the paintings of Charles Russell (1864-1926), an artist praised for his "keen brilliance" in this article. Form study groups around specific paintings, investigate the imagery carefully and critically, and compare Russell's portrayal of cowboys to Draper's.

- Draper refers several times to the $71 billion cattle industry in this country—a topic certainly worth researching. Thus, focus on specific aspects of this industry, such as environmental impact and nutritional trends, and then revisit both the ideal and the real world of cowboys.

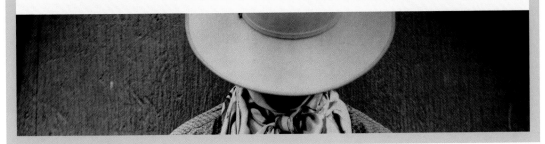

INDIAN: SCENES FROM A RENAISSANCE

While native peoples have been decimated, oppressed, and neglected for centuries, Joseph Bruchac finds signs of renewal even on reservations. Focusing on the ways in which native cultures are recovering, he also considers their place in, and contributions to, contemporary American culture.

As you read "Indian: Scenes from a Renaissance," you should consider the following questions:

- If you were asked who Americans are, would you automatically include Native Americans?
- If you were asked who Native Americans are, how would you reply?

PASSING THE TORCH *On snow-frosted plains near Green Grass, South Dakota, Chief Arvol Looking Horse imparts the moral teachings of the Lakota Sioux to his relatives. He is the 19th in a succession of keepers of the sacred White Buffalo Calf Pipe, a talisman that confers the honor of spiritual leader. In past generations, many Indian religious practices were banned by the U.S. government and later restricted by a lack of access to sacred sites and ceremonial objects. The American Indian Religious Freedom Act, enacted in 1978, guarantees Native Americans the right to worship freely.*

INDIAN: SCENES FROM A RENAISSANCE

Photographs by Maggie Steber

THE HEALING TOUCH *David Little Wounded reaches out to calm a friend on South Dakota's Cheyenne River Indian Reservation, where wild mustangs have been reintroduced after an absence of 140 years. One tribal program uses the horses as therapy to treat substance abuse, and David says the animals helped tame the wildness in him too: "Working with horses just brings out your inner peace."*

THE SPIRIT OF THE RESERVATION IS CHANGING.

THE BALANCE OF TRADITION AND PRACTICALITY

IS BRINGING THE CULTURE TOGETHER FULL-CIRCLE.

I'd come to Cheyenne River looking for something good: the same spirit of revival and hope that I'd heard about in Indian communities across the United States, from the stone-cold canyons of Manhattan to the quietest hogan in the desert Southwest.

From the top of Coffee Butte in the land of the Cheyenne River Sioux, you can see 50 miles in every direction. As I circled my gaze, I could see black dots on the wide, grassy plain below. Buffalo. I picked out one herd, then another, another and another. A herd in each of the four directions: good omen.

"Look," said Dennis Rousseau, of the tribe's Game, Fish, and Parks Department, "over there."

I followed his stare to a group of brown specks on a ridge, two miles to our east. "Wild horses," he said. "Coming our way."

I watched as perhaps a dozen animals flowed toward us down the slope, smooth as rushing water. They were half a mile away, led by a brown stallion, head up, alert to any danger. Sure enough, distant as we were, the stallion caught wind of us. He stopped abruptly on top of a hill, stared, then turned, driving the horses before him, out of sight as quick as the flash of a hawk's wing.

Wild horses are back on the reservation after an absence of 140 years, trucked in from Nevada, where they were being shot at and killed by poachers only a few years ago. Their return, like seeing buffalo in all directions, was enough to stir the blood of at least one old East Coast Indian: me. For the first time in generations, "the buffalo, the elk, and the mustang are all back on the reservation," said Dennis, lowering his binoculars. "One of our holy men told me that means something really good is going to happen."

I'd come to Cheyenne River looking for something good: the same spirit of revival and hope that I'd heard about in Indian communities across the United States, from the stone-cold canyons of Manhattan to the quietest hogan in the desert Southwest. In a thousand

Adapted from "Indian: Scenes from a Renaissance" by Joseph Bruchac: National Geographic Magazine, September 2004.

LIFE ON THE REZ *Children get lessons in calf roping as Sunday afternoon winds down in Tuba City, Arizona, on the Navajo Indian Reservation. The reservation, at 25,500 square miles—about the size of West Virginia—is the nation's largest. The Navajo Nation has about 250,000 members, more than half of whom live on the reservation.*

whole landscapes seem raw with the memory of what went on here in the late 19th century. This is the land of the Custer campaigns and the Ghost Dance, where Lakota Sioux resisted the coming of the whites and the loss of their sacred lands with every beat of their hearts. Sitting Bull's grave is out here.

Approaching Cheyenne River after sundown, I hit the search button on the radio and landed on the biggest station around—KLND, Indian owned and operated—just in time to catch a dedication. "For all you lovebirds out there, whether you're snaggin', shackin', or married," said the deejay. "Here's Lil' Kim!" If nothing else, young Americans of all colors have music in common: 50 Cent and Eminem are just as popular with Indians as they are with other American kids. Short hair, tattoos, and baggy pants are everywhere you look. Even adult men who used to wear shoulder-length hair have gone to the buzz cut, in a quiet revolt against Indian stereotypes.

A while later, at my motel, I tuned in channel 30 on cable and saw an ad from Emmanuel Red Bear—who also goes by the Lakota name of Tatanka Iyotake, the same name as his great-great-grandfather, Sitting Bull—making it known that he is a certified Lakota language instructor, an experienced emcee for powwows, honorings, and giveaways, and is also available for suicide counseling and gang awareness workshops. It was a vision of hope that made me sit up in my chair.

The next day I caught another glimpse of hope, this time in black and white. On the wall of Dennis Rousseau's office hangs one of those reservation maps I've grown familiar with over the years, showing the checkerboard pattern of lands once reserved for Indians. Today about half of the original 2.8-million-acre Cheyenne River reservation is in tribal hands; the rest was expropriated by federal allotment acts between 1887 and 1934 and sold to whites. But the tribe is making a huge investment in its future by seeking a federal loan to buy back 22,140 acres, including the grazing land where their buffalo herd now roams.

small ways, that revival—cultural, political, economic, spiritual—may wind up transforming the lives of 4.1 million Native Americans, the vast majority of whom today live somewhere besides a reservation.

And yet, as I'd driven across South Dakota to get here, I'd expected this place to be different. Confined to some of the driest, most unforgiving real estate in North America, Sioux reservations on the Great Plains are among the poorest in the country. Just south of Cheyenne River, people on the Pine Ridge Indian Reservation live on a third of what the average American earns and are three times as likely to be jobless. They also commit suicide twice as often. In this part of America,

With more than 3,000 animals, the Cheyenne River herd is the largest tribally owned buffalo herd in America, and one of the best managed. Tribal biologists, for example, plant micro chips in young buffalo to identify and monitor each animal from a command post in Rousseau's office. Some of the animals are sold commercially, but most of the meat, which passes USDA inspection, goes to schools and other tribal programs such as the Elderly Nutrition Center, part of an effort to reintroduce buffalo meat, which is leaner than beef, as a staple of the reservation diet.

Long-term, says Dennis, the goal is to reestablish buffalo culture on the reservation, with benefits both practical and spiritual. "The buffalo, which is sacred, is still providing for us by giving us a paycheck and putting food on the table," said Dennis. "Nature put the buffalo on this Earth for a reason. So I guess it's come full circle."

Full circle. That's an apt metaphor for the state of Native America in September 2004. For more than a century, Indians in the United States survived in the white man's shadow by humbling themselves, becoming invisible, learning to survive, if barely, on handouts from the federal government. Inevitably, the fabric of Indian communities, their dignity and identity, were left as shredded and thin as the few remnant buffalo herds on the Great Plains, ghostly reminders of a rich and glorious past.

Today that situation is changing as Indians across the U.S. exert new influence over their lives and their communities. One of the most visible signs of change is what some call the "new buffalo"—the casino, which for better or worse has become Indian country's most potent symbol of economic empowerment, mostly due to the success, and notoriety, of gaming tribes like the Mashantucket Pequot in Connecticut,

> The buffalo, which is sacred, is still providing for us by giving us a paycheck and putting food on the table.

whose Foxwoods casino will gross more than a billion dollars this year.

Other tribes have followed the Pequot and opened casinos of their own: Hon-Dah and Apache Gold in Arizona, Feather Falls in California, Cherokee Casino in Oklahoma. Still, only 40 percent of federally recognized tribes run gaming operations, and not all Indian casinos earn substantial income. Even those that do are subject to the oversight of nontribal bureaucracies at both the state and federal levels. Many Indians also question the long-term viability of gaming, which depends, like a fad, on the tastes of a fickle public.

With this uncertain future in mind, the Oneida Nation of Wisconsin has directed casino profits toward tribal development and used them to buy new land, pave roads, and even build an elementary school in the shape of a huge turtle, revered by the Oneida. "A generation ago our children went to school in old clothes and were taunted by the kids who were better off," says Bobbi Webster, the tribe's public relations director. "Today those other kids are jealous."

The Oneida are also diversifying their portfolio. With three other tribes, they founded Four Fires, a business consortium designed to explore opportunities beyond gaming. Their first joint venture is a 43-million-dollar hotel near the National Museum of the American Indian, opening this month in Washington, D.C. Embodying the renaissance in Indian country, this museum, which houses one of the world's largest collections of Indian art and culture, was funded in part by millions of dollars in casino revenues, donated by tribes like the Pequot and Oneida.

The Chippewa of northern Minnesota went a different route, investing half a million dollars of their casino profits to revitalize the mainstay of their traditional life: wild rice, an annual aquatic grass that grows only a few places in the world. One of them, happily, is Nett Lake on the Bois Forte Chippewa reservation—the largest contiguous wild rice lake in the world, where native people have been gathering *manoomin* since the time of the ancestors.

Historically the rice harvest brought this community together, kept it intact, and provided a major source of income. However, in the 1970s and '80s outside growers with new methods drove the price to a fraction of what the Indians were getting. Bois Forte rice production also waned as Nett Lake became overgrown with reeds and other vegetation. That changed in 2003, when the tribal council decided to allow motorized barges and cutting equipment, paid for by casino money, onto the sacred lake to clear out the sedges, bulrushes, and water lilies that had created bogs and choked off the flow of water needed to grow rice.

To see how the restoration was going, I paddled out onto Nett Lake one morning with Ron Boshey and his 32-year-old son, Barry Day. Once we were clear of the shore, Ron pulled a cigarette from his pocket and stripped off the paper. Then he balled the tobacco in his hand and sprinkled it over the water as he spoke a few words of Chippewa.

"Just a little offering to the Great Spirit," he explained. "Asking for a good harvest."

Leaning hard into his pole, Barry sent us cruising silently into the nearest rice bed, which rippled like a wheat field in our passing wake. Then he steered us into a patch where the rice grains were ripe brown. Ron reached out with a pair of slender wooden sticks, called knockers, which he used to strip rice into the bottom of the canoe, moving his arms with the fluid grace of a tai chi master. Soon the canoe was filled with long quills of rice. I noticed other boats moving in the reeds nearby, and I felt as if we'd all hit the jackpot.

I was on a train clattering south along the Hudson River, heading toward a place as Indian as anywhere in the United States: New York City. Famously traded to (or stolen by) the Dutch in 1626, New York today is home to more than 85,000 Native Americans. About 85 percent of Indians in the United States now live off the reservation, and every large city in the U.S. has its own Indian community. This is partly due to a government relocation program, begun in 1952, that sent thousands of Indians around the country in search of work.

Brad Bonaparte is one of these urban Indians, a 42-year-old Mohawk artist and ironworker whose father and grandfather walked the high steel with wrenches and welding torches, making the city's skyline. Every workday he puts on a brown hard hat bearing the insignia of an eagle feather, a potent symbol of blessing and protection worn by many Mohawk ironworkers.

Brad remembers admiring the World Trade Center from his apartment in Jersey City. "I used to see those towers at night, and always thought how cool it would be to have the job of changing the lightbulbs on the antenna." After the towers came down on 9/11, Brad was one of the many Mohawk who worked to clear the debris and search for remains, putting in 12-hour days for three and a half months. And like everyone else working in the ruins, Brad's crew soon carried burdens heavier than concrete and steel.

"Every kind of priest was there, from the Catholics to the Buddhists, but there was no one for us Indians. One day we heard there was a tobacco burning ceremony a few blocks away, at the New York branch of the National Museum of the American Indian, so we all just walked off the job and went there." It helped. A few days later Brad's crew found the radio tower he'd dreamed about. "I ended up standing on it," he says, "but not in the way I thought."

For Brad and many thousands of other Indians, Native identity is a growing source of strength that helps them cope with the mainstream America that flows all around them. Yet it can also be a source of turmoil. I speak from personal experience: Like many Native Americans today, my heritage is mixed. My mother was Abenaki, my father was Slovak, and it didn't really dawn on me that I was Indian until I was in my teens. Even then, it took a long time for my own mother to accept that I was the first of my family in three generations to go "public," to seek out relatives and elders who could teach me the stories and language my Abenaki grandfather never shared with me. For a while my mother referred to me as, "My son, the Indian," until my younger sister Margaret asked, "But Mom, what does that make you and me?"

Good question. Such confusion, often laced with self-hatred, is surprisingly widespread, even in communities where Native blood predominates. "Are you proud to be Lakota?" I heard a Sioux man ask a six-year-old on Pine Ridge Reservation, in South Dakota. "Nuh-uh, I'm not a Indian," the little boy said before running away.

That anxiety, like so much that impedes Native Americans, is a legacy of U.S. government policies. For half a century the tone of Indian education was set by government boarding schools such as the Carlisle Indian Industrial School in Pennsylvania, founded in 1879 by Richard Henry Pratt, a U.S. Army officer whose philosophy was "Kill the Indian and save the man." Schools like Carlisle removed Indian kids from their families at an early age; some were kept until they were adults. If they spoke their native languages, they were severely punished. No wonder, then, that today surprisingly few Indians speak their native tongue or know much about their own traditional culture.

Tom Porter is an elder of the Mohawk Nation living in upstate New York whose grandfather and great-grandfather both attended the Carlisle School. He remembers the gray-faced men he knew as a child: "When they came home, they were just like a computer that has no feelings." He never heard his grandfather speak a word of Mohawk, one of the Iroquoian languages.

By 1997 about 5 percent of Iroquois still spoke their native tongue; of those, most speakers were in their 70s and 80s.

A NEW GENERATION *Byron Billie and JoJo Dakota Osceola, both full-blooded Seminoles, changed into typical teen garb after winning awards for native costume at a Seminole cultural fair in Davie, Florida. Though immersed in mainstream youth culture, "I most definitely identify more with my Indian heritage," says Byron. JoJo hopes to become an attorney specializing in Indian law.*

Concerned that the Mohawk were on the verge of losing their language altogether, Porter initiated what he calls a "Carlisle School in reverse" to jump-start his own personal Indian renaissance in a new Mohawk community. Called Kanatsiohareke (meaning "place of the clean pot"), Porter's community offers several two-week immersion courses in Mohawk language each summer, taught by fluent speakers.

The results, though modest, are measurable. Forty or more students take the courses every summer, including several dozen or so who have become fluent enough in Mohawk to speak at ceremonial occasions. One day as I watched a language class, I noticed that one of the instructors, Bonnie Jane Maracle—whose Indian name is Iehnhontonkwas—looked younger than most of her students. "I'm one of the 2002 graduates," she said, beaming. "A few years ago I could barely talk Mohawk, but now I've learned enough to teach the Mohawk phonics class."

The Cherokee Nation, with tribal headquarters in Tahlequah, Oklahoma, also offers language immersion classes to help preserve Cherokee culture. The courses are based on a syllabary developed by the Cherokee's peripatetic genius, Sequoyah, in the early 19th century that helped the Cherokee to become the most literate of Indian nations, with its own newspapers and schools. The Cherokee also developed political skills that they sharpened in the 1830s, as leaders such as Chief John Ross lobbied Congress, in vain, against the forced removal of 16,000 Cherokee from tribal homelands in the southeast U.S., culminating in the infamous Trail of Tears.

Today, in a clear sign of renewal, the Cherokee are again showing their gift for cultural and political sophistication—a balance of tradition and practicality that has helped them endure the near-death experience of their expulsion to Oklahoma, the periodic land-grabs and neglect of the U.S. government, and a litany of other injustices, from a lack of potable water to anti-Indian demagoguery in Congress.

Led by Principal Chief Chad Smith, the Cherokee Nation runs a dynamic lobbying program, with a full-time office in Washington that deals with government's convoluted bureaucracies—ranging from Congress, which writes the federal laws governing relations with Indian tribes, to the Bureau of Indian Affairs, which administers U.S. policy. Smith himself spends a lot of time in Washington calling on legislators and federal agencies, and notes that the American Indian experience seems to run in cycles—"adversity, survival, adaptation, and occasional prosperity—over and over."

I looked for signs of Indian renewal all over this country, and I found them, but I kept coming back to buffalo. One buffalo in particular. I saw him only once, in South Dakota months ago, but he's with me still, like a recurring dream.

Dennis Rousseau and I were out in Sioux country, where Sitting Bull led his band of survivors toward a vision that only he could see. Just before sunset Dennis and I decided to drive out in search of the buffalo herd one more time, just for the fun of it.

As soon as we left the main road, we were surrounded by prairie dogs. Their burrows dotted the landscape on both sides of us, their quick whistles raised the alarm from hill to hill. A round head poked up out of one burrow, swiveled toward us, ducked out of sight. A burrowing owl materialized, followed by the wide wings of a ferruginous hawk. Both were hunting for prairie dogs. The hawk passed; a mead-owlark popped up from the grass and flew in the opposite direction. It was as if I'd traveled back 200 years, to a time before the slaughter, the plows, the heavy hooves of cattle.

Then a wind kicked up, blowing dust across the grass. For a moment the land looked like a yellow ocean rippled by waves.

Dennis nodded. "The buffalo will be coming down here into that wind," he said.

"Facing into the storm?"

"Cattle," Dennis said, "just let the storm push them. But not buffalo. They know there's an end to the storm, so they go into it."

"Like Sitting Bull did," I said.

"That's right," Dennis said. "That's right."

Soon we saw a solitary bull, head down, pushing forward against the weight of the wind. We followed him over a small rise and found ourselves in the midst of hundreds of buffalo. Young bulls, calves, yearlings, cows. They were peaceful and fully alive, charged with a power that seemed to flow from the old, enduring earth itself. Dennis took this in, gave me a look.

"The wonders," he said, "of buffalo."

Discussion Questions

- Throughout the article, references to and images of circles and cycles recur. What meanings and values are associated with these circles and cycles? How does the way in which the article unfolds, from beginning to middle to end, express these values and meanings as well?

- While the term "Indian" is, of course, a notorious misnomer, and while "Native American" has become a widely used alternative, in what ways does the word "American" prove problematic, too?

- Continuing with this theme, do you see comparable difficulties with "Latin American," "Asian American," "African American," and so on? In comparison with these identifications, does anything about "Native American" make it distinctly problematic?

- Even as Bruchac mentions the stereotyping of "Indians" several times, he does not detail what those stereotypes are. Nonetheless, can you piece them together from between the lines--and/or from your own exposure to and knowledge of images of "Indians" in the United States? How, and why, was Bruchac's self-image as a child affected by such views?

Writing Activities

- The theme of language and identity, which is prominent in this article, comes up elsewhere several times in this reader (see, for example, "Changing America," "Once Upon a Time in Laredo," and "ZipUSA: Pawtucket, Rhode Island"). What specific quandaries do native peoples face when it comes to their native tongues and native identities? How do these compare with, say, those of young people who are not versed in the native tongues of their immigrant parents?

- Insofar as one's ethnic background contributes to shaping one's identity, which aspects of that background are the most crucial, and why? Conversely, to what extent, and in what ways, do the perceptions of others affect who we are, or would like to be?

- What can one gain by identifying oneself as an "American"? What can one lose?

- "The wonder of buffalo": what does that simple phrase at the end of Bruchac's essay capture and express? In the process of addressing this question, you may well find it helpful to learn out more about the natural history of the American buffalo, and perhaps also that of the wild horse.

Collaborative Activities

- Casinos come up several times in this article, and while Bruchac tends to treat them favorably, there is, in fact, considerable debate about them in this country. Delve further into this debate, as well as into the broader question of legalized gambling. Where do you stand on the issues?

- Given the oppression to which native peoples have been subject in the past, do you think they deserve special prerogatives today? What about other ethnic groups who have suffered discrimination, and worse?

INSIDE THE PRESIDENCY

Prompted by the swearing in of Barack Obama as the 44th President of the United States in January of 2009, journalist Elisabeth Bumillor looks at traditions and practices that have remained constant over the last few decades regardless of who occupies the White House.

As you read "Inside the Presidency," you should consider the following questions:

- Before reading the article, consider the expectations its title arouses. As you read, do you find it satisfying these expectations?

- In the process, consider also the qualities of the exposé genre in both serious and tabloid journalism. To what extent does this article conform to either or both?

Washington, D.C., a new President is inaugurated

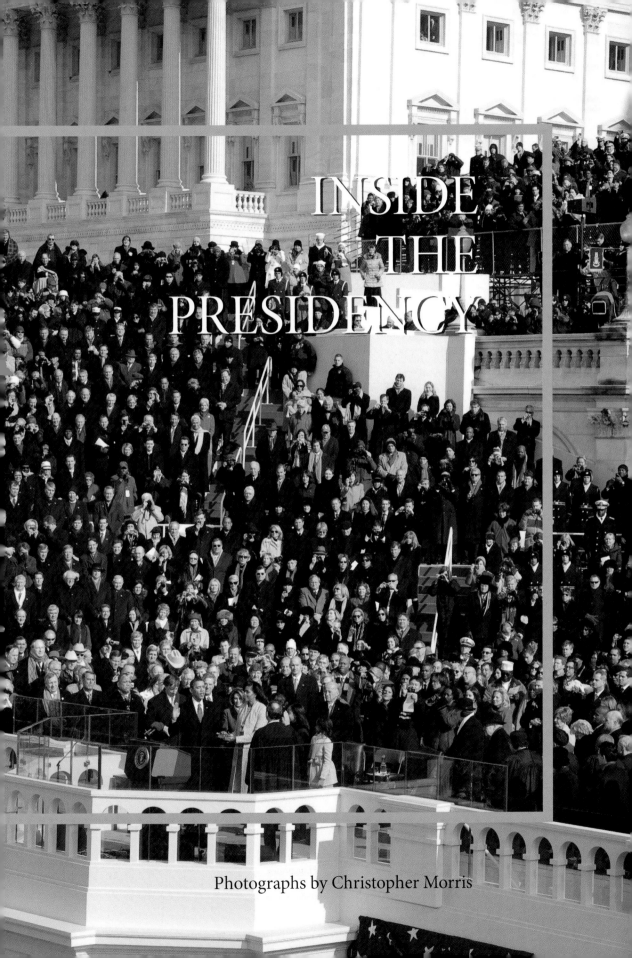

INSIDE THE PRESIDENCY

Photographs by Christopher Morris

The Lincoln Bedroom in the White House

AS POLITICS AND PRESIDENTS CHANGE,

CONTROLLED CHAOS AT THE WHITE HOUSE REMAINS THE SAME.

THANKS TO THE STAFF, CHANGES AT THE WHITE HOUSE ARE SEAMLESS TO BOTH THE PUBLIC AND THE RESIDENTS INSIDE.

First families move in and out— They get a four or eight-year lease.

History always makes a sharp turn in Washington when a new american president takes the oath of office, and so it will once again on January 20, 2009. There will be new Cabinet members, a new Congress, a new foreign policy, a new style in the East Wing, new embarrassing relatives (if the past is any guide), and new first friends.

But many other things in the private world of the President of the United States will stay remarkably the same. The maids on the permanent White House housekeeping staff will make the presidential bed, just as they always have. The kitchen staff will still peel potatoes and scramble eggs. The gardeners will have planted 3,500 tulip bulbs to bloom in the Rose Garden in the spring.

The permanent care and feeding of the President of the United States is an industry staffed by hundreds of people, largely supported by taxpayers, and little understood beyond the gates of 1600 Pennsylvania Avenue. First families move in and out—"They get a four- or eight-year lease," says Gary Walters, former chief usher of the Executive Mansion. But the staff, customs, and mechanics surrounding the world's most powerful chief executive endure, often for generations.

Walters knows this well. As a deputy manager and then manager of the most famous address in the U.S. for 31 years, from Gerald Ford to the second President Bush, Walters spanned six presidencies and crises both global and domestic until his retirement in 2007. He ran a house with a 90-member residence staff of butlers, maids, chefs, maître d's, elevator operators, florists, curators, carpenters, electricians, and plumbers. In some ways it was like running the world's most exclusive hotel, except that Walters was in charge of a building with four major and often conflicting functions: home, office, grand museum, ultimate event site. Incredibly, the White House has welcomed up to 30,000 guests in a single week.

Walters, an Army veteran and a former officer in the old Executive Protective Service (now known as the Secret Service Uniformed

Adapted from "Inside the Presidency" by Elisabeth Bumiller: National Geographic Magazine, January 2009.

Division), brought military precision and the utmost discretion to a job that was never 9 to 5. His worst times, he recalls, were when one first family moved out, typically around 10 a.m. on January 20, and the other moved in—by 4 p.m. the same day.

Walters's goal was to have the departing family's possessions out and the new socks in dresser drawers, personal furniture arranged, pictures hung, family photos displayed, favorite snacks in the kitchen—all in that six-hour time frame. There is no chance to get a head start, since the new President does not officially take office until January 20 at noon, two hours after his moving van pulls up under escort in the White House driveway as the outgoing President leaves for the Capitol. To make the deadline, Walters would deploy the entire 90-member staff at once, divided into teams with specific tasks. Months of planning included repeat verbal dry runs. (No such rehearsals took place before Richard Nixon's early departure, however. Word went out that the First Lady had made a request through the usher's office for packing boxes. "That's how we knew," said Betty C. Monkman, a former White House curator.)

Some transitions were especially rocky. Bill Clinton stayed in the Oval Office until 4 a.m. on January 20, 2001. "Then he had his desk that had to be cleaned out," Walters recalls. He had to wait until the President went to bed before he could swoop in and help Clinton's staff clear out the office to make way for George W. Bush.

But once things settle down, "the White House is first and foremost a family home," Walters says. "It is the responsibility of the residence staff to change to the needs of every family, and not pigeonhole the family to the White House."

To ensure such comfort, Walters would begin questioning the First-Lady-to-be after the election in November, as soon as the outgoing President had invited the new one to visit. What rooms would you like to use for your bedrooms? What time do you want to get up in the morning? What kind of toothpaste should be in the bathroom? What snacks would you prefer stocked in the pantry?

Bush 43 said pretzels, which got him into trouble in 2002, when he choked on one while watching a football game in his White House bedroom, lost consciousness, hit the floor, then came to, with only the presidential dogs as witnesses. Bush's father requested easier to swallow Texas Blue Bell ice cream. He did not, however, request pork rinds, despite making a regular-guy show of nibbling them in public. "It was totally bogus," Walters says. "He didn't eat them."

The second Bush also liked to keep a stainless steel water dish at the foot of the South Portico's curved granite staircase, and Dale Haney, the superintendent of the White House grounds, could be seen moonlighting as the walker of the presidential terriers, Barney and Miss Beazley. Chelsea Clinton had her friends over for pizza in the State Dining Room. Susan Ford hosted her junior prom in the East Room. In the Reagan Administration, known publicly for its old Hollywood glamour, the President and First Lady liked their private, just-the-two-of-them dinners served on trays in front of the television.

So what's for dinner? First Ladies and Presidents generally haven't cooked at the White House, although they have a second-floor kitchen in the family quarters, separate from the main kitchen on the mansion's ground level. The Clintons liked to use their kitchen for post-party glasses of champagne and raided its refrigerator for leftovers. But most families have simply selected a weekly menu from choices offered by the White House chef. State dinners, barbecues for Congress, and holiday receptions for the diplomatic corps are paid for by taxpayers, but the President is billed for all food consumed by his family and his personal guests. In the first months of a new administration, sticker shock is routine.

Preparations for a formal dinner in the East Room

"I can't remember anybody not complaining," Walters says, recalling in particular Rosalynn Carter's astonishment at the size of the bills. "Mrs. Carter came from Georgia. Things were a little cheaper there at the time. But let's face it, you've got world-class chefs. The garnishes they put on foods, the way they dress them up, it's like eating in a restaurant."

Food comes from various Secret Service–approved commercial suppliers, but also from farmers markets and occasionally just the grocery store. Sometimes the White House chef will stop in at a local butcher on the way to work and pick up a last-minute chop for the President's dinner. Wine, always American—the White House stopped serving French wine in the Ford Administration—comes directly from the wineries and includes offerings from Virginia and Idaho as well as California. (White House Francophile customs

died hard: Mamie Eisenhower once had her favorite apple brown Betty listed on a state dinner menu as *Betty Brune de Pommes.*)

The first family pays its own dry cleaning bills, although the staff takes care of sending out the clothes to high-end establishments in town. The President's shirts are done inhouse, as are all the family's sheets and towels. The President's valet keeps his shoes shined and deals directly with the housekeepers to replace missing buttons. Presidents select their own suits from the closet each day, although staff members have been known to reject presidential ties as too busy for television. "I can't think of any President who had somebody else pick out his clothes," Walters says.

When the President leaves the White House, he travels within an enormous, ever secure bubble, whether seated in

Presidential motorcade driving up to Air Force One

the armor-plated limousine referred to internally as "the Beast," flying on Air Force One, or sleeping in one of the 600 to 800 hotel rooms required for each stop on a foreign trip.

The President's road show includes a caravan of White House staff, State Department officials, Secret Service agents, communications technicians, crews for *Air Force One and Marine One* (the presidential helicopter), Department of Defense staff, and press. A big foreign trip typically includes up to 800 people, among them 30 White House staff members, more than a hundred members of the Secret Service, and some 150 representatives of the media—television and radio correspondents, camera crews, sound technicians, print journalists, wire service reporters, and still photographers.

The group is actually transported in two planes: *Air Force One* for the President, his staff, his Secret Service agents, and a small pool of reporters in the back; and the White House press charter, usually a United 747, for the rest of the media. (Reporters are rotated in and out of the 14 press seats on Air Force One, but on either plane, media organizations pay dearly for the seats, typically the price of first-class airfare or more.) The entourage is accompanied by cargo planes that transport the President's limousine and a spare, plus sometimes *Marine One,* to each stop.

The nucleus of the bubble, referred to within the White House as "the package," consists of the President, his senior staff, the Secret Service detail assigned specifically to him, and a small pool of reporters. The package essentially isolates the President from the rest of the bubble and the outside world. Inside the package life is serene; humming outside is the 24/7 infrastructure required to keep the peace.

The head of the road show in the Bush 43 Administration was Joe Hagin, former deputy chief of staff in charge of operations, who believes in striking a balance between protecting the President and allowing him some exposure in public. "You can't lock him in a steel box and move him around," Hagin says. "You have to get him out."

Hagin would begin planning Bush's foreign trips up to a year ahead. Every November or December, he'd sit down with the White House chief of staff and national security adviser to block out what usually amounted to five or six annual presidential trips overseas. Some were built-in, such as the yearly Group of Eight meeting of industrialized nations or the NATO summits, both must-attends for the American President. But others, like Bush's trip to Africa in February 2008, were designed to highlight administration policies and to show the White House flag.

"My geography's not good enough to do it without a map," Hagin says. So with maps unfolded all over the conference table in the national security adviser's office, and with the Air Force One pilots on hand to consult, the group would figure out what stops made geographic sense. There were all-important political considerations as well. Bush 43, who grew increasingly unpopular overseas as his administration progressed, often augmented his European trips with stops in former Soviet bloc nations like Albania, where he could count on pro-democracy, pro-American crowds to cheer him on.

The White House Communications Agency, or WHCA, builds its own communication system for each destination, and on foreign trips the leader of the free world can push a button on the telephone in his hotel suite and be instantly connected to a direct-dial U.S. system. Bush hasn't carried a personal cell phone for security reasons, but he had access to any number of them while traveling.

Presidents come and go. Butlers stay.

One cell is specifically for the presidential limousine, where there is never a problem with background noise. People who have been inside say that the limo is eerily serene, as if the outside world were on mute. The President can see the crowd, but he can't hear it, especially not over the deep rumble of the Beast's big V-8.

Air Force One is the President's refuge. He can sleep in his cabin, a suite in the nose of the plane with a shower and two daybeds. Or he can work out; before Bush's knees gave out and he abandoned running, he had a treadmill set up in the Air Force One office on foreign trips. The jet's kitchen serves full dinners prepared by military stewards, but they are unlikely to win culinary or nutrition awards. Steak, chicken, and pork chops are normal fare. In June 2002, when Bush was on a trip to Florida to promote dietary and physical fitness, the Air Force One lunch menu, printed on gold-edged cards for all passengers, was corned beef sandwich, steak fries, and strawberry cheesecake.

As the President moves with ease from meeting to meeting, an intense choreography churns around him, all outlined in hundreds of pages of briefing books. "We can go to the other side of the world and land precisely to the minute," Hagin says. "But you've got to know what you're doing. These trips are not for the faint of heart." Only experienced staff members go overseas, and they are expected to know where to stand, what to wear, how to address foreign dignitaries, and when, literally, to run.

In spite of the briefing books and the overall efficiency of Hagin and his team, travel foul-ups occasionally occur. In May 2005, only a malfunction in a live hand grenade, tossed into an ebullient crowd of tens of thousands in Tbilisi, Georgia, averted what could have been a lethal attack. In 2004, Bush waded on

The White House, Washington, D.C.

his own into a group of security agents to pull a Secret Service agent out of a shoving match with the Chilean police. In 2002, the Beast came to such a sudden stop en route to lunch in Beijing with then-President Jiang Zemin of China that the wire services reported a blow-out, conjuring images of Secret Service agents rummaging through the trunk for a jack. The problem was in fact mechanical, and the President was moved to the spare limo within moments.

Not surprisingly, the President, like everyone else, is happy to get home. Although Ronald Reagan said he often felt captive in the fishbowl of the White House, many other Presidents and their families have loved it there.

And why not? There is, after all, a recently refurbished movie theater, suitable for viewing major Hollywood films sent overnight from the studios. (In the past couple years Bush saw *The Kite Runner* and *The Perfect Game*.) There is a swimming pool, the same one where Gerald Ford spoke to the press in his bathing suit. There is a tennis court, too, and the Children's Garden, a shady spot created by Lady Bird Johnson, its walkway lined with bronzed handprints and footprints of presidential grandchildren.

Most of all, there is a sense of home and history, coupled with the knowledge that a first family, however well cared for and fed, can only pass through. Or as one of the permanent household staff gently reminded Barbara Bush during her time as First Lady: "Presidents come and go. Butlers stay."

Discussion Questions

- How would you characterize the tone of the article? What about the diction? How are they related to the author's purpose? What do they suggest about her attitude to her subject?

- "Few outsiders ever see the President's private enclave," writes Brumillor. Does the article make us "insiders"?

- What do we learn about the staff of the White House? What don't we find out? What do you think is more significant?

- What do the presidential anecdotes that pepper the essay indicate about the presidents themselves? Do they provide significant insight into their characters?

Writing Activities

- Compare the domestic life of the president as described in this article with his traveling life. What are the similarities? What are the differences? What are the implications?

- Is the security and, in some cases, secrecy that surrounds the president compatible with the idea of a "free society"? On the other hand, is the idea of a "free society" compatible with the reality?

- Insofar as a president represents the United States to other countries, what qualities do you think he, and perhaps eventually she, should embody? What, if any, of these qualities are specifically "American"? Do some transcend national differences?

- "The personal is political": How does this phrase, originally used by feminist critics in the late 1960s, resonate with regard to the presidency today?

Collaborative Activities

- In some ways, this article raises as many questions as it answers. Identify several and consider their significance. Do you think they could or should be addressed?

- Do you think it right that "the permanent care and feeding of the President of the United States is an industry staffed by hundreds of people, largely supported by taxpayers"? Insofar as taxpayers do support this "industry," do they have a right to an accounting? Should the public be involved in determining what's a reasonable expense or lavish excess?